Praise for
How NOT to Practice Social Work

As an educator, I found this book extremely helpful. I thought this book could only be used by students of Social Work. But I was wrong! This book is for anyone in a position dealing with people. As an educator, I am aware of the fact that I have to understand "how to make myself more purposely influential in every area of my life." My students will be better students when I am willing to bust through my mental road blocks and enhance my teaching skills. The author, Eva Forde, did a splendid job breaking down what Social Workers, as well as anyone dealing with people, need to do to be better at their profession.

Margaret Howard, MSE, Educator

How NOT to Practice Social Work is the active practitioner's reminder that we, too, are valuable and deserving of our own focused, loving self-care and that it is and will always be of crucial importance to operate within an ever evolving professional, ethical framework.

Marie Sparkes, Practitioner

I'm faced with 2 dilemmas. Firstly, I know that as much as I praise this book, it could never parallel how good it actually is and secondly, I owe a friend an apology after saying nonfiction books are too boring to tolerate. This book is so cleverly and empathetically written that I found myself highlighting whole pages and bookmarking every chapter. The relevance that "How NOT to Practice Social Work" equates to your everyday routine is significant enough to make a positive impact in your life even if you begin the first page with very little expectation. I promise that you'll gain a lot more than you bargained for.

M. Lovelace Julien, Medical Student and Writer

D1369866

This book speaks of freedom, which all thinking people will cherish. This freedom which I think Eva espouses comes into view from the first chapter to the last: be aware, consider the costs, keep informed, apply systems, be proactive, be open and real, appreciate even the 'dull and ignorant', respect the rules and be a channel for love.

Anthony Hutchinson, Educator

Bravo!!!!!!! Excellent! Excellent! Excellent! I really enjoyed reading each section. It is a well needed manual that details all of the essential components needed to be an effective and efficient social worker. It is a self care survival reference guide.

Katrina Jones, Host of *Positively Affirmative* Blog Talk Radio, Inc. program and coach at *ProsperityLiveCoach.com*

How NOT to Practice Social Work is filled with answers to a lot of unspoken questions and feels like you have your own personal life coach who has a wonderful sense of humor by your side. I should know. I bought the Kindle version and everyone thought I was reading a novel. It got so good I had to buy a hard copy so I could highlight the parts that I love in all my favorite colors so I can share it every chance I get. It's a really good guide for a profession that guides others. Well done!

Lyrris Williams, Social Worker

I enjoyed every sentence in this book! Definitely worth the read. To get humour and depth from a book about Social Work is not very easy, but Eva you did it. Your awesomeness is all over it!

Shamoy Hajari, Social Worker and founder of Jamaica School for Social Entrepreneurship (JSSE)

Thank you for writing a book that addresses the key issues Social Workers face in the field as they try to practice at global standards. The book is truly a must read for ALL Social Workers. It's beautifully written, easy to read, and everyone who reads it – including those who are not within the profession – can find principles that will improve their standard of practice in their own field.

Kimone Clarke, Social Worker

How N O T to Practice Social Work

Saving Good People From Bad Practice One Step at a Time

Eva W. M. Forde

How NOT to Practice Social Work: Saving Good People From
Bad Practice One Step at a Time

Copyright © 2012, 2013 by Eva W. M. Forde

Cover illustrated by Nelton Johnson; Saadiyah "Butterfly" Smith,
Editor

This book is dedicated to my 12-year-old self.

I love you.

You're OK. And don't worry; everything is going to be great!

Acknowledgments

For the journey and the lessons, God, I am grateful.

There are so many people to thank; people who provided support, direction, encouragement and guidance even when they may not have been aware of the significance of what they did at the time.

Thank you to my predecessors and teachers at each level of my growth and development, including my social work professors at Oakwood and Columbia Universities as well as great minds like Eckhart Tolle, Wallace Wattles, James Allen, Napoleon Hill and Anthony Robbins that have provided fundamental information.

There are also people whom, in my life, have been foundational pillars of guidance and strength. Those who are now living whom I would like to acknowledge are my supportive parents, Winton and April Forde; my amazing godparents, Jocelyn and Claude Thomas; Gilbert and Georgia Allen, my parents in Jamaica, and my Uncle Nathan and Aunt Ruth Forde. Thank you for loving me and accepting me in spite of myself. Your examples are with me daily and I love you.

To Mason and Shamica West and "my kids"; my daughter, Odile Blake; my brothers and their families: Winton and Velma, Wayne and Darcel and Sean; Vincent Squire, Ken Eady and Derek Quashie; Marlene and Donovan Lennox and the rest of my wonderful family in Jamaica; Jada and Evon Williams, my adopted siblings; Nelton and Simone Johnson, Joi Dunn, Nicole Meltzer, Dr. Sammy and Mrs. Mary Browne, members of my Master Mind group: Omar, Antonn, Carl, Sebastian, and Alvin; Marie Sparkes and Albert Richards; Suzonne and Tom Murrell, Venice and Raymond Irving, Laverda and Andrew Thomas; Kirkland Pratt, Karen Lu Fang, Doug McCaffrey, and Jonathan Burke, THANK YOU!

I cannot forget the legacy of my mother, Yvonne Joy Forde, and grandmothers who have prayed for me. I love and miss them, but their prayers resonate from the universe and are what helped make this book possible.

Finally, I would like to acknowledge my former students whom I am proud to call colleagues in the field of social work practice. I thank you for challenging and accepting me. Continue to gain knowledge, seek truth, and promote justice.

Here's to the promotion of professional social work!

Don't wish it was easier; wish you were better. Don't wish for less problems; wish for more skills. Don't wish for less challenges; wish for more wisdom. — Jim Rohn

Table of Contents

Foreword

We all agree that your theory is crazy, but is it crazy enough? — *Niels Bohr*

Social *What?*

Ask the average Joe on the street what they know about social work and you might hear something like:

"Social *what?*"

"Social workers give food to poor people who can't feed their families."

"Aren't they like psychologists?"

"They help poor people on welfare."

"Aren't they like psychiatrists?"

"You go to a social worker if you have to go to court, and they tell the judge what they think you should do."

"Aren't they like sociologists?"

"Social workers think they can save the world."

"I used to date a social worker. She was constantly trying to figure me out and make me get in touch with my feelings and change me."

(Hey, how'd my ex get in here?)

Or, my personal favorite,

"Social workers take children away from their families."

While all of these answers reflect a general concept of an activity that a social worker might do (and some inadvertently), none of them accurately conveys the core of what social work is or aims to accomplish and, in fact, these widely held generalizations only help to perpetuate feeble views of the profession (not to mention wreak havoc on one's dating life).

So, what *is* social work?

Webster's online dictionary defines social work (n) as:

Any of various professional activities or methods concretely concerned with providing social services and especially with the investigation, treatment, and material aid of the economically, physically, mentally, or socially disadvantaged.[1]

The National Association of Social Workers (USA) states that

"The primary mission of the social work profession is to enhance human well-being and help meet the basic needs of all people, with particular attention to the needs of those who are vulnerable, oppressed and living in poverty" (NASW, 2011)[2].

That being said, ask any recent social work graduate what social work is and they'll tell you that there's a world of difference between what the books *say* and what you actually *do* – what goes into making social work *work*. That's because social work is less of a thing that can be statically defined and more of an experience that must be… well…experienced. It's an art and a science with as many nooks and crannies to perspectives and interventions as there are scenarios in the human experience; a recipe, of sorts, for making better conditions for us all.

There is no higher religion than human service. To work for the common good is the greatest creed. – Woodrow T. Wilson

---

[1] http://www.merriam-webster.com/dictionary/social%20work
[2] http://www.socialworkers.org/nasw/naswbrochure.pdf).

It's a philosophy

I've recently finished reading a wonderful book titled *The Slight Edge* by Jeff Olson. In it, Olson makes the argument that performing incremental, simple tasks over a long period of time will ultimately improve one's overall state of affairs. With that being said, what I loved about the book and took away from his discussion was a new attitude— a strategic way of thinking and approaching any task at hand. It almost didn't matter how much good information people possessed, he said. If they didn't have a way to process it all, it was useless. That process, he believed, was one's philosophy.

Let me be clear. We're not really talking about the discipline of philosophy that supposes and hypothesizes about the "isms" and "schisms" of the world, but, as defined by the *Miriam-Webster Dictionary,* about "the most basic beliefs, concepts, and attitudes of the group."

The things that are easy to do, he says, are also easy *not* to do and, therefore, most of us don't do the little things that, when done consistently over time, have the power to determine our success. It's not a novel idea, but a practical one that encourages discipline, persistence, and quality.

Similarly, anyone who decides to study social work and then goes so far as to gain a degree in the thing has made an agreement to adopt a certain social work philosophy. This philosophy not only concerns the things a social worker does, but includes an agreement of what that person represents; a buy-in of sorts to a kind of moral high road of thoughts and actions even when off the proverbial clock.

Of course I'd be lying if I said that every social worker in the world thought exactly the same on every issue, but I think it's pretty fair to say that while we may not all drink from the same glass, we're all drinking the same water.

So, what's this book about anyway?

Ninety-nine point nine percent of Social Work literature (true statistic, of course) is quite formal in its composition of information, as it should be. Professional social workers must take their craft seriously in order to protect and promote the scientific integrity of what they do, right? Social work is a vocation that already struggles to maintain credibility in several professional circles, and the expertise of our skill is challenged in intellectual settings all over the world.

Well fire up the griddle and pull out momma's good china, 'cause this book falls squarely in that .01% of social work literature that is *not* wholly scientific, but is rather matter-of-fact-here's-what-it-is banter. Many of the examples used are anecdotal, and subjective perspectives are incorporated to make the points as relevant as possible.

That being said, don't expect a literary masterpiece to unfold before your eyes (though a New York Times #1 Best Seller wouldn't be bad).

How NOT to Practice Social Work is my version of a colloquial and sometimes irreverent, yet educational look at what makes social work a profession in its own right by considering, primarily, what it's *not*.

And so for starters, social work is NOT…

- just an experiment in helping the less fortunate or mentally ill.
- taking away happy children from their loving parents.
- giving away old clothes that you'd never wear yourself.
- dolling out free food stuff to poor people.
- giving your friend advice about a problem they're having.
- sitting in an office psychoanalyzing "the crazies" all day long.

On the other hand, social workers …

- work wherever people are and wherever there is discrepancy in fair treatment or social justice.
- take pride in their ability to strategize and execute interventions that ultimately benefit others.
- see themselves as powerful change agents that right wrongs, champion causes, and serve with passion.
- have a strong commitment to social justice and progressive change.

- will remove vulnerable children from environments that threaten to compromise their human development such as abuse, neglect, abandonment, or maltreatment…and we don't apologize for this one bit.

Social work is for those who have, themselves, experienced the power of their own humanity and have humbly embraced the truth that we are all one, that we all have value and worth, and that as we take up the call to empower others, we empower ourselves and we better the world.

I hope you enjoy reading *How NOT to Practice Social Work* as much as I have enjoyed writing it. I have a good feeling about you and I believe you'll either make a great social worker or, after having read this book, be able to spot a bad one a mile away.

Here's to the promotion of professional social work!

Introduction

Your profession is not what brings home your paycheck. Your profession is what you were put on earth to do with such passion and such intensity that it becomes your spiritual calling. — *Virgil*

I love social work.

I love belonging to a profession whose sole purpose is to help people and make the world a better place to live.

I love being able to qualify what comes naturally to me with scientific evidence.

I love the diversity of the profession—the people, arenas of practice, and scenarios.

I love sharing the life-stage with like-minded people who also want to see the world be better.

I love being allowed—mandated even—to acknowledge my own handicaps and deal with them professionally.

I love having enlightened social work friends to lean on.

I love the energy that social workers generate when they're in a room together. It's electric!

I love that social work encourages me to explore my interests to be more than "just" a social worker.

I love that social work acknowledges that I am a fallible human being, with needs and biases and influences and perspectives that must be recognized if I'm to be of any good to anyone else.

I love that I've found my calling and that my profession, like me, is ever evolving, ever unfolding, ever changing.

I love who social work has helped me to become and who it encourages me to be.

What I don't love is bad practice....

Part 1: The Person

Chapter 1

Unawareness:
The Key to Self Mastery

As long as the ignorance of the self lasts, so long will there be misery.—
Tripura Rahasya

Unawareness: Not a Pretty Sight

Am I the only one who has ever witnessed a well-dressed person oblivious to the toilet paper stuck to the bottom of their shoe, ever trailing behind them as they walked as if to say, "Look at me, look at me", or had the uncomfortable experience of talking to someone with food stuck in their teeth, spittle around the corners of their mouth, or a booger dangling precariously from their nose?

Yeah; not a pretty sight, but yet a magnificent portrait of unawareness.

The sad part is that if these examples were the worst consequences social workers had to face, we would have little to concern ourselves about.

But for the social worker, the toilet paper is repressed anger, the wedged broccoli is unethical practice, the spittle is undefined boundaries, and the booger is burnout. Can you see how unawareness in any of these areas can be more than a little distracting?

Social Worker, Know Thyself

There's actually only one lesson to be learned in this chapter, and that is this: know thyself.

He who knows others is learned;
He who knows himself is wise.
—Lao-tzu, Tao te Ching (sixth century B.C.)

And since we're talking about self, let me offer a bit of self-disclosure at this very critical juncture…on second thought, I'll save it for therapy (notice my self-awareness here).

In the meantime, let's explore the significance of self-awareness.

Only by much searching and mining are gold and diamonds obtained, and man can find every truth connected with his being if he will dig deep into the mine of his soul. – James Allen

Self Awareness: it's important

Here's the thing about social work practice: you've got to be well within yourself before you can be well for the client.

This understanding of self is such a fundamental component of practice that it's got to be understood early enough in the process of social work education so as to be ingrained within the subconscious efforts of the practitioner.

Let me say it another way.

You must actively seek to improve yourself through the process of analysis of your*self* (i.e. the part of you that is, at its core, your true spirit). *Self* is the primary tool of the practitioner. As you better your*self*, you become more effective in your use of *self* to help better the client.

Ok, last one.

You know when you're on a plane and the flight attendant instructs that in the unfortunate event that the plane loses cabin pressure, oxygen masks will drop from the ceiling, and that if you have children or persons who need assistance next to you that you should secure your own on your face first before attempting to assist anyone else?

Well, it's like that.

You can't help anyone else put on their oxygen mask if you're dead now, can you?

No, you can't.

So, the same principle applies in the helping world: you can't most effectively help people when you, yourself, are suffocating in an airless sea of unresolved issues and ongoing denial of unawareness. Eventually you'll smother and die a slow and painful social work death, otherwise known as burnout, and that's never a good look.

The tool of your trade

Just as the mechanic uses a wrench, the chef uses a spatula, and the artist uses an easel, the self is the tool the social worker uses to do his or her work.

And just like a mechanic tunes a car for the journey, a chef sharpens his knives for carving, and an artist primes his canvas for painting, the social worker must take time out to service his or her soul tool so that he or she can get the most out of its performance. This is where the self-analysis and soul searching come in. This is where you give your spirit the space and time it needs to be calm and still. This is the essence of self.

Man is a tool-using animal. Without tools he is nothing. With tools he is all. – Thomas Carlyle

~ ~ ~

Professional social workers know that tools that don't get a tune up or repair will eventually wear out.

~ ~ ~

Who are you anyway?

The universal question that we all ask at one time or another is "Who am I?" Sometimes it's asked as "Where did I come from?" and sometimes the question is "What is my purpose?"

However it's asked, at the heart of the question is the desire to know ourselves. Unfortunately, many of us don't take the time to find out and the alternative is confusion and manifested frustration because of it.

Start to think of yourself less as a body with a spirit, and more as a spirit with a body.—Deepak Chopra

There is no relationship of greater importance to achieve than the relationship between you, in your physical body, right here and now, and the Soul/Source/God from which you have come. If you tend to that relationship, first and foremost, you will then, and only then, have the stable footing to proceed into other relationships. Your relationship with your own body; your relationship with money; your relationship with your parents, children, grandchildren, the people you work with, your government, your world . . . will all fall swiftly and easily into alignment once you tend to this fundamental, primary relationship first. —Abraham-Hicks

My, what a powerful self you have!

Allow me to get a little philosophical here.

Your "self" is a powerful and dynamic energy, able to influence a conversation or decision, channel an emotional response, and interpret meaning and intent from other selves it comes in contact with.

Most of us take our power and influence for granted, but the aim of social work education is to teach the social work student how to recognize and actually use one's self as a powerful tool for positive change. When this is done successfully, the social worker remains a humble yet confident agent of social transformation, able to help save lives, restore families, and possibly balance a checkbook.

The Flip Side

However, when learners don't fully grasp this principle, their clients stand in danger of any number of negative outcomes. This could range from the rejection of needed case management services to succumbing to the feelings of helplessness within them.

There's nothing worse than an unaware helper—except if they're unaware *and* obnoxious—but we'll save that discussion for another time.

As long as you think you're green, you'll grow. As soon as you think you're ripe, you'll rot. — *Scott Horton*

The Self Test

Since we're meant to be talking about how NOT to practice social work, let's get back to how to tell when you could use some help for yourself. See the following list and check the ones that speak to you.

☐ You find it difficult or uncomfortable to take criticism, even when it's constructive

☐ You find it easier to criticize rather than praise or applaud others or yourself

☐ You are constantly distracted with painful memories of the past

☐ You don't find enjoyment in things you used to; in fact, it's hard to find enjoyment in most things

☐ You feel lost, stuck, or immobilized

☐ You find yourself busy, but not able to get much accomplished

☐ You're facing a major life change (like having a child or going through a divorce)

☐ You have anger, anxiety, or self-esteem challenges

☐ You find yourself depending on prescription meds or alcohol to get through the day

☐ You find yourself telling your capable clients what to do rather than helping them to come up with solutions

☐ You find that a current situation in your life is negatively taking up a large amount of your thinking and emotional processes

If you answered "yes" to any of the above, get support – but not before you finish reading this chapter.

An ongoing process

Self-discovery is an ongoing, never ending process, but unless you begin the journey – deliberately tending to the wellness of your spirit – you may find yourself frustrated and disillusioned with, not only your life, but your ability to successfully impact another's.

As human beings, our greatness lies not so much in being able to remake the world ... as in being able to remake ourselves. —
Mahatma Gandhi

Don't rush it

And because it's a lifelong process, you needn't be daunted if you feel like you're stuck or not making any progress. It's all part of the journey to continue to evolve into the person you are meant to be, and so far you're probably doing alright.

Confront the dark parts of yourself, and work to banish them with illumination and forgiveness. Your willingness to wrestle with your demons will cause your angels to sing. Use the pain as fuel, as a reminder of your strength. — August Wilson

What to do, what to do

I won't spend time in this book looking at all things that go into self-analysis, soul searching and your spirit, but if it's been a while since you got a tuning, consider the following strategies to help you get your groove back.

1. Give yourself the gift of therapy.
   ...or get a coach or professional supervision. Actually, this is more of a directive than a suggestion, so just do it.

2. Be still and meditate.
   Get quiet and clear your mind of all thought. Relax. Breathe. There are several good products to teach you how to do this effectively.

3. Be honest with yourself.
   Around 97% of our thoughts are subconscious. Get curious about your motives and desires, your fears and biases about everything — especially the stuff you don't want to deal with or admit to — and use your conscious thought to get to the bottom of what makes you tick.

4. Take a big boy/girl approach.
   Take ownership for what's not working and make a commitment to take the steps to change for the better.

5. Don't be afraid to give yourself credit for the good things in your life; after all, you've created them.

6. Play.
Remember that thing you love to do? Make time to do it more often and get lost in the joy it brings you. Pay attention to how good it makes you feel and notice how it impacts areas of your life afterwards. Repeat.

7. Ask yourself some questions and allow the answers to lead you to seek support for your self:
Where am I spiritually?
Why did I get into this profession?
Am I really being good to myself? What could I do (or let go of) to improve?

~ ~ ~

Smart social workers know it's not smart to avoid your personal issues.

~ ~ ~

The truth about people who seek support

Sometimes getting support for your self looks like confiding in a trusted friend that can listen and provide a balanced perspective. Sometimes it's taking time alone to mediate and center your inner soul.

If you're religious it might look like reading some spiritual literature or going to a place of worship. And sometimes, yes, it may look like checking yourself in to the nearest psychiatric ward – usually right around the time you start to see little green men circling your cubicle.

The truth is you don't need to be going through a crisis or "crazy" to seek support through informal channels or therapy or counseling. Think of it as self maintenance.

A friend of mine once put it like this: Therapy is a gift you give to yourself. Barring therapy, find a healthy outlet or coping mechanism that not only helps you to deal with your issues, but helps to move you to the next level of self-awareness and understanding like yoga or meditation, self-help literature, a support group, coaching, or physical exercise.

Here are just a few tips suggested for the smart social worker on the forward journey of self-awareness:

1. Forgive yourself. Another way to say this is, be compassionate with your self. It's okay to be you and, in fact, it's the only option you have! Sure, you might mess up a time or two, but who doesn't? It's all part of a grand learning process and, in that case, you're doing just fine.

2. Be open to constructive criticism – or any criticism for that matter. Analyze your feelings about what's being said. Get perspectives from your trusted confidants about the validity of the information and make adjustments if necessary.

3. Acknowledge your mistakes and apologize when you've done something to hurt someone or cause damage to a situation, even if inadvertently. Take note of any emotional or intellectual insights gained along the way and use them to grow.

4. Move on. Let it go. Forgive others quickly. Don't hold grudges. They only make you constipated and wrinkle faster.

Demand of yourself

Let's be honest, we all have had challenges in the area of self-mastery from time to time (and if you haven't, call me and tell me your secret). It's not always easy, but unless you work at learning the truth about who you are – the essence of you, your desires, goals, likes, fears, and why they exist – you'll be incapable of helping your clients to move to self-mastery and discovery for themselves. Moreover, you'll be an incomplete version of your best self. Who wants that?

Insistence on persistence

Over the years I've come to value the principal of persistence, so that now I accept anything to be achievable based on that premise alone. I sum it up in the catchy phrase, "insistence on persistence." But I rush to qualify that this insistence isn't one of struggle or strain at all. Rather, it's an expectation at the deepest level – an innate "demand" or "order", as it were, to settle for nothing less than what I want.

I insist!

Insist from yourself

Insistence takes on many forms. When it comes to self-awareness and mastery, insistence of your *self* is a never ending process of self-reflection and forgiveness. When I'm in a funk or just can't seem to get myself motivated to be positive, calm, or loving, I consider the truth that those qualities are my natural state and I *insist* for myself the acceptance of these.

Insist on acceptance with where you are (mentally, physically, emotionally, and spiritually), forgive yourself for any shortcomings you may feel you have, and move forward with hopeful anticipation knowing there's always more to know, more to experience, and more to become.

Sometimes insistence means insistence on behalf of others (like respect for boundaries and standards), but unless you know your *self* – who you are at your core – you'll be limited in your ability to insist anything of anyone else in a meaningful way (didn't I just say this?).

I insist on the truth. I surround myself with people who tell the truth. – Shelby Lynne

One more thing

Since I started my conscious journey into the self I've been amazed at how *un*conscious I had been living and how challenging it really is to make the effort every moment of every day to be mindful of the truth.

And the truth is that I'm a co-creator with God (Universal Life Force, Infinite Spirit, Providence, Allah, Jehovah, or whatever you choose to call that higher power) in my reality.

The annoying clients?
I helped to attract them.

Those frustrating delays?
I helped to create them.

That unsatisfying salary?

Yep; even that. I helped to create all of it, and on some level, I want it because I choose to focus on it.

Now, whether or not you choose to believe this for yourself is irrelevant. But if you do grasp this, you have access to unlimited power to change your perception and change what you create in your future. See, if you accept that you helped create some things that you decide you *don't* want, you can use that same energy to create circumstances, situations and events that you actually *do* want. This is why I'm so determined to focus my mind on what's right in the world, what's right in my clients, and what's right in the future. Focus on anything less will just bring more of the same.

Learn from the greats

If you want to be good, follow good examples; but if you want to be great, follow the examples of the great. Here are just a few:

Retire into yourself as much as possible. Associate with people who are likely to improve you. Welcome those whom you are capable of improving. The process is a mutual one. People learn as they teach. —Seneca

Everyone thinks of changing the world, but no one thinks of changing himself. — Leo Tolstoy

We are the only beings on the planet who lead such rich internal lives that it's not the events that matter most to us, but rather, it's how we interpret those events that will determine how we think about ourselves and how we will act in the future. —Anthony Robbins

Look well into thyself; there is a source of strength which will always spring up if thou wilt always look there. — Marcus Aurelius

To be nobody but yourself in a world that is doing its best to make you just like everybody else means to fight the greatest battle there is to fight and to never stop fighting. — E. E. Cummings

The journey of true success and lasting leaderships begins with the inward journey to the soul. — James Arthur Ray

Your vision will become clear only when you look into your heart. Who looks outside, dreams. Who looks inside, awakens. — Carl Gustav Jung

We must strive for freedom if we strive for self-knowledge. The task of self-knowledge and of further self-development is of such importance and seriousness, it demands such intensity of effort, that to attempt it any old way and amongst other things is impossible. The person who undertakes this task must put it first in his life, which is not so long that he can afford to squander it on trifles. — George Gurdjieff

What we know matters but who we are matters more.— Brené Brown,

The key

Read this chapter again. Read it several times, if necessary. Read it until it inspires you to take action, and when it does, read it again so that you get into the habit. Remember, information is useless until it's put into practice, so what are you waiting for?

For the record, self-awareness:

- Is an ongoing, lifelong process (it's continuous and never stops)
- Influences our self-worth and actions/decisions which, in turn, influence our practice
- Carries with it responsibility to act
- Benefits our clients
- Is gained through
  - ✓ Meditation and being still
  - ✓ Listening to soothing music
  - ✓ Solitude
  - ✓ Observation and reflection
  - ✓ Dreams
  - ✓ Discussions with people we trust about ourselves
  - ✓ Knowing our likes and dislikes
  - ✓ Exploration of different activities
  - ✓ Contemplation of our various roles (as parents, teachers, learners, advocates, etc.)

A man after my own heart

One of the authors I hold in great esteem is a man named James Allen (1864-1912). He is most notably remembered for his work entitled *As a Man Thinketh* (1902) where he beautifully articulates the power of the human mind to shape one's destiny. However, the implied or otherwise less talked about principle is that in order for a person to maximize the use of his or her mind, one must become present; one must become aware. This awareness or attentiveness to the present moment can be evoked from one's depth of revelation into his or her own infinite origin.

A man becomes calm in the measure that he understands himself as a thought evolved being, for such knowledge necessitates the understanding of others as the result of thought, and as he develops a right understanding, and sees more and more clearly the internal relations of things by the action of cause and effect he ceases to fuss and fume and worry and grieve, and remains poised, steadfast, serene.

The calm man, having learned how to govern himself, knows how to adapt himself to others; and they, in turn, reverence his spiritual strength, and feel that they can learn of him and rely upon him. The more tranquil a man becomes, the greater is his success, his influence, his power for good. — James Allen

Chapter 2

At All Costs
Avoid Personal Therapy

In Hollywood if you don't have a shrink, people think you're
crazy. —Johnny Carson

True Story

Want to know the quickest way to burnout, a sure-fire formula to jeopardize the wellbeing of your clients, and make your coworkers avoid you like the plague?

Step One: identify your issue. You know; the thing you need counseling or therapy for and, Step Two: avoid it.

Don't do anything but ignore that big counterproductive hot pink elephant in the room.

In fact, go on making the same mistakes over and over until you end up in a screaming match with the police who have to drag you kicking and screaming from your office in defiance. Seriously, it doesn't have to be so dramatic. But, believe it or not, that is exactly how a former supervisor of mine ended her career with our agency.

Just pitiful.

Prerequisite

There's a popular saying in social work that the people who go into the profession need professional help the most.

Ha-ha; very funny.

While this may be closer to the truth than many would like to admit, the study of social work has within its realm real healing power not only for the client, but essentially for the practitioner.

To its credit, the profession calls on its members to act with integrity, and at the heart of acting with integrity is recognition of one's own baggage and a call to unpack!

> *Don't bring baggage from an ex relationship into your next relationship…unless you want it to be a short trip.* – Robert Tew

Unconscious Programs

Psychologists have long known that as much as ninety-seven percent of our thoughts are subconscious and that these are what drive our actions. Well, if this is true then it stands to reason that much of what has been programmed into our subconscious is not what we would have adopted had we understood its impact on us to begin with.

> *The chains of habit are too weak to be felt until they are too strong to be broken.* – Samuel Johson

Think about it: would you speak the language you do if you hadn't been programmed to do so when you were a child? Would you enjoy the type of music or food that you grew up on had it not been automated in your experience? How about your confidence, your biases, or your fears? Think those all just popped up out of the blue or can you grasp that they were most likely learned through your experiences and interactions with your environment?

It's true. Most of us are nothing more than a bundle of mechanized thoughts, feelings and emotions parading as if we're independently thinking and acting evolved beings. We often miss the fact that we have the power to choose our thoughts and feelings in every moment, as opposed to reacting habitually to stimuli when it presents itself.

Man is made or unmade by himself. By the right choice he ascends. As a being of power, intelligence, and love, and the lord of his own thoughts, he holds the key to every situation.—James Allen

So, when someone compliments us we can choose not to be flattered just as surely as we may make the choice to react otherwise.

But that example's innocuous.

The real threat happens when we as helpers allow our unconscious, predisposed, programmed thoughts, beliefs and biases to run our lives and, in turn, impact the lives of our clients.

But social work challenges all of that.

Psychology 101

One of the things I love about social work is its eclectic nature and, in this case, its respect for and utilization of the principles of psychology; and fundamental to psychology is the concept of mental health. For the social worker this is especially essential because we work with people all day, every day – many of whom are not in the best mental health themselves.

Now, you tell me, how unlikely would it be to watch a sea urchin teach a starfish how to swim, or a turtle teach a snail how to run? That's what we call "the blind leading the blind," and yet those are great analogies of what happens when we well-meaning, trained professionals neglect to look after our own states of mind and emotional wellbeing. If I've said it once, I've said it a thousand times: 'you must be well for yourself before you can help your client to be well. '

~ ~ ~

The smart social worker safeguards their clients by first safeguarding themselves.

~ ~ ~

Changes

Let me be clear. Being well for one's self is not a static experience. You don't just exercise today and then never need to exercise again in life; or clean house now and expect it to last for a lifetime. Life itself is a dynamic and evolving process of change and growth and there will always be elements that challenge your sense of balance and homeostasis. The key is to seek support through these changes while we grow and expand into the best individuals and helpers we can possibly be and look for opportunities to improve.

An ounce of prevention

And who said you need to be going through a crisis to seek support and improve? In fact, if you're not seeking support on a regular basis, you're bound to encounter an overwhelming crisis sooner or later. However, the more you make counseling, therapy and/or coaching a regular part of your maintenance regime, the less likely you are to experience crisis in a debilitating form. And if it's true that an ounce of prevention is worth a pound of cure, then a month of support can change your entire life – and your client's life too.

Therapy is a gift you give to yourself. – Marie Sparkes, Gestalt Therapist

I've bought into the argument that I must look out for my own wellbeing before I can look out for anyone else's. This makes sense for two reasons.

First, if I'm not well, how can I help anybody else? Would you go to a sick doctor? Probably not.

Second, when I'm taken care of, I can better take care of my family and my clients. By looking out for myself I reduce the chances of malpractice or harming others. Besides, people seem to like me better when I'm not turning into the Incredible Hulk.

Supervision

Partner in the fight against bad practice is the superhero Supervision.

~ ~ ~

Supervision is the secret weapon of the smart social worker.

~ ~ ~

Just like Superman's job is saving earth from total destruction by would-be villains, supervision's role is saving social work from utter futility by would-be bad practice methods.

Really, this tool should be the first "given" for the social work professional; and for the social worker the term aligns more with mentoring than with management.

Unsupervised practice is our kryptonite; we're not meant go it alone. Social work is founded and reliant on the interdependence of people, so if you remove that dynamic, it's just not social work – not good social work anyway.

Got supervision? – Seen on a social work button

Exceptions to the rule

Now, I'm fully aware that many great social workers don't have formal supervisors – often these people are retired or more mature in their practice and would have had years of supervision already – but I'll bet my bottom dollar that they do have trusted mentors, allies and confidants that they consult on a regular basis for the things that come up in their practice and lives. Show me a good social worker and I'll show you his friends, 'cause good social work just doesn't happen without it.

For Your Own Good

In lieu of a therapist, counselor ,or coach, a skilled supervisor can help you work out many of the kinks in your professional practice as well as offer you guidance and support for personal concerns. Generally, this person is a professional social worker themselves with enough practice skills under their belt to comfortably provide leadership, direction, and accountability. And while it helps to have good rapport from the start, it may be a quality of the supervisory relationship that has to be nurtured and developed over time. The important thing is to have a support, a sounding board, a confidant that you can run decisions by and dump emotions on if needs be.

> *Mentoring is a brain to pick, an ear to listen, and a push in the right direction. – John C. Crosby*

The B Word

A critical function of a supervisor is to help the professional social worker avoid the dreaded villain (cue the suspense music)…burnout.

Burnout is a very real phenomenon in the helping professions. Many of us have experienced it, and,if we're honest, can identify ways in which we contribute to it in our practice, often times burning the practice candle at both ends until it's…well….out.

The dictionary defines burnout as physical or mental collapse; the "experience of long-term exhaustion and diminished interest." One practitioner described it as a total loss of energy mentally, physically and emotionally, and researchers warn that generalist practitioners suffer the most risk of burnout – up to 40%.

It makes sense. The very nature of our jobs makes us prime candidates for monthly psych evaluations and mental health days, and depending on the area of social work you may find yourself in, the demands can be dreadful physically, mentally, and emotionally.

~ ~ ~

Professional social workers know there's a thin line between sanity and insanity.

~ ~ ~

Confession Time

I'm not proud to admit it, but I've experienced burnout at least once in my professional career (and maybe more, but who's counting?). Looking back on it now, I can tell you that I contributed to my demise through lack of organization, lack of self management and lack of supervision. And the crazy thing was that I knew intellectually that my practice wasn't up to snuff, but I felt almost powerless to do much of anything about it.

See, the problem with burnout is that it so thoroughly evaporates your energy and drive that it can be terribly difficult to even open your eyes to see the steps to get out of it, much less to take them. Not only was I miserable, but my clients suffered from my resulting poor practice.

Eventually I found my mojo, left my very draining job, and have been on a crusade against bad practice ever since.

Danger, Will Robinson

In the years since my burnout episode I've learned a lot about the triggers and red flags to pay attention to so that I never reach that stage again. If at any time I see myself getting even a little off track I've conditioned myself to say, "Danger, Will Robinson! Danger, Will Robinson!"

If you were raised on cheesy American 1970's television series like I was, you may recall a show called *Lost in Space*. In each episode the main character, Will Robinson, would inevitably face some life threatening trouble and be alerted by his trusty robot with the alarm, "Danger, Will Robinson! Danger, Will Robinson!"

Psychologists Herbert Freudenberg and Gail North have theorized that the burnout process can be divided into 12 abstract phases, and I can attest to their soundness from my personal experience. While these phases provide a general schema leading to burnout, should you find yourself experiencing more than a few of these symptoms, consider yourself in danger, Will Robinson.

1. A compulsion to prove oneself

2. Working harder

3. Neglecting one's own needs

4. Displacement of conflicts (the person does not realize the root cause of the distress)

5. Revision of values (friends or hobbies are completely dismissed)

6. Denial of emerging problems (cynicism and aggression become apparent)

7. Withdrawal (reducing social contacts to a minimum, becoming walled off; alcohol or other substance abuse may occur)

8. Behavioral changes become obvious to others

9. Depersonalization (life becomes a series of mechanical functions)

10. Inner emptiness

11. Depression

12. Burnout syndrome

~ ~ ~

Smart social workers know that every flame of glory eventually burns out.

~ ~ ~

Dos and Don'ts

If more than a few of those symptoms look familiar, it's well past time for you to seek the support of your nearest therapist, counselor, or supervisor, and while you're at it, book a month-long vacation ASAP. If you feel like you might be experiencing burnout, make sure you do the following things:

- Seek out personal, professional therapy.
- Explore various healthy techniques to help you cope with stress.
- Include coping techniques in your *daily* routine.
- Exercise regularly.
- Maintain a support system of people who build you up, not tear you down.
- Spend time nurturing your hobbies and the personal interests that inspire you.

But make sure you don't:
- Blame others or avoid getting the help you need and deserve.
- Neglect your spiritual self.
- Let your job consume you.
- Neglect your family for the sake of your job.

- Avoid your personal issues – the ones you've tried to avoid.
- Neglect to make time for yourself.
- Depend on antidepressants or alcohol to ease your pain.
- Stop having fun.

The Last Resort

When all else fails, get out.

I don't mean that you should get out of the game of life, so you can put the bottle down. What I mean is that you may need to consider leaving your current work, relationship, or perspective for that matter, in order to get back to your center – your truth and where you feel most balanced – and your dharma in life.

The word dharma is a Sanskrit word that means purpose in life. I learned it during one of my there's-got-to-be-more-to-life-than-this tirades. According to the law of dharma, we each have a unique purpose in life that is best achieved through expressing our true selves; but when we're off balance, tired, and feeling stuck there's no way we can fulfill our purpose, or respectively, be fulfilled ourselves.

Don't let guilt or the money you're making keep you stuck in a position where you're miserable if at some point you decide where you are is not where you want to be. You'll do yourself, your clients, and your family a huge disservice the longer you stay upset. Not every battle can be solved with schedule changes or rationalization. Sometimes you may have to know when your path has run its course. A good therapist or clinician can help you sort out your affairs and realize that you always have options.

~ ~ ~

The smart social worker knows that it's better to get out than to burn out.

~ ~ ~

You, yourself, as much as anybody else in the entire universe, deserve your love and affection. — Buddha

Chapter 3

Don't Educate Yourself

Education's purpose is to replace an empty mind with an open one. —
Malcolm Forbes

Educate yourself

Hey!

Did you hear the one about the social worker who stopped learning after she got her degree?

She got fired.

~ ~ ~

Smart Social Workers expose themselves to knowledge
before their lack of it exposes them.

~ ~ ~

What's in Your Diet?

Depending on where one works your regular literary diet could be as mundane as going over client records (which may be about as exciting to read as watching paint dry), or as depressing as reading *The Diary of Anne Frank*, Alex Haley's *Roots*, and John Steinbeck's *The Pearl* – in that order!

Some social workers may get a chance to hear the daily headlines which at least keeps them up to date on peripheral current events. Still others may be given credit for staying informed in their specific area of expertise through journals, blogs, or magazine subscriptions.

With the ambush of managed care and constant modifications to legal rulings, the million case scenarios and the situational considerations that never end, social workers have got to stay informed. It's not enough for them to have a general clue – they've got to have the right ones. Many times social workers are the only people in the room looking out for the client's interest. When this happens, we can find ourselves in some very influential circles where our voice matters – and if it doesn't then our job becomes to make sure that it does.

Anyone who stops learning is old, whether at twenty or eighty. Anyone who keeps learning stays young. The greatest thing in life is to keep your mind young. —Henry Ford

We now accept the fact that learning is a lifelong process of keeping abreast of change. And the most pressing task is to teach people how to learn. —Peter Drucker

An education isn't how much you have committed to memory, or even how much you know. It's being able to differentiate between what you know and what you don't. —Anatole France

Education is a progressive discovery of our own ignorance.—Will Durant

The best contribution one can make to humanity is to improve oneself.—Frank Herbert

Some people drink from the fountain of knowledge, others just gargle.—Robert Anthony

The only person who is educated is the one who has learned how to learn and change.—Carl Rogers

A Good Lesson

I had a teacher in graduate school who, on the first day of class, said to us that she took it for granted that we read the New York Times on a daily basis. She argued that if we were to work in an international field like social work within the diversity-charged city of New York, we had better avail ourselves of as much information as possible and pray to God we never got caught with our preparation pants down.

Now, I've done my fair share of teaching, and from a lecturer's perspective, I can totally relate. It was often times a challenge to get my students to read the assignments, much less outside of class, so I find her argument quite relevant – I just don't find it practical.

Get Real!

Let's be honest. It's impossible to keep up to date on every topic important to social workers at all times – our profession is just too broad and too diverse for that. Besides, information overload is never a good look.

~ ~ ~
Professional Social Workers know the difference between being informed and being inundated.
~ ~ ~

However, we do agree that it's important for the professional social worker to maintain a basic awareness of major tenants and important developments in his or her field of practice, and generally on major social work movements.

The quandary, it seems, lies inherent in the profession itself. Social work *is* so broad and *is* so diverse, and in the world of generalist practice, there's no end to the issues that can come up.

A multiplicity of options

In fact, part of what I love about social work is the fact that with a bachelor's degree you can work with children, the elderly, in schools, with an employee assistance program, in a hospital, in policy development, in communities, in law enforcement, and in a host of other areas.

There's almost no end to social work's reach. But let's be realistic about how we can manage our knowledge base and still maintain some semblance of sanity.

What we know for sure

So, let's talk about what professional social workers *do* know. Professional Social Workers know that:

You're never too old to learn.

Your first degree qualifies your learning, not justifies your cessation of it.

Social workers are not know-it-alls, but are always open to new knowledge, new viewpoints and new ways of thinking.

Professional journals are our friends.

Self-help books, tapes, and seminars are good for you.

Each one of us has something to contribute to the profession's database of information.

Attending conferences and seminars is NOT a waste of time.

Not all information relative to social workers is found in social work literature, so it's important to read outside of our profession's works.

The more aware we are, the better equipped we are to serve our clients.

There is such a thing as too much information; and the old adage your grandmother used to say is still true: 'everything in moderation.'

Do as I say, not as I do

I'll be the first to admit that I rarely watch the news or listen to the news stations on the radio. There's something about the bombardment of negative information that I'm allergic to.

So a few years ago I made a conscious decision to disengage from the practice because each night after consuming more than my fair share of a menu of rising inflation, inclement weather, and unsolved murder mysteries, I found myself feeling distraught, helpless, and depressed. It was like a soap opera – leave it for a few months and when you come back it's like you never missed a thing.

I decided not to surround myself with the problems, but to spend my time and energy on the solutions.

We cannot solve our problems with the same thinking we used when we created them – Albert Einstein

Side note: In all of my practices, I make it a point to feel good for myself so that I can be well for the people around me, and I'm sorry, but the nightly news does *not* put me in the best of moods.

Instead, I took up listening to news briefs in the mornings or going through the newspaper on the weekend. I had electronic updates sent directly to my BlackBerry so during the week I was able to read the headlines as often (or not) as I wanted. That way, I would have control over what I digest and what I throw away.

You know what I found after a few months? I discovered that I was no worse off than any of my counterparts. I spent that extra time in the pursuit of specialized knowledge –

specifically, that of personal development, which not only helped me personally, but helped me to provide better service to my clients. Interestingly enough, as I cleared my life of the constant barrage of information thrown at me daily and enlisted techniques to manage that onslaught, I made space for clarity, calmness, and proficiency in essential areas of my life and work.

Perfect!

So how does one cultivate a passion for learning beyond the classroom when there doesn't even seem to be enough hours in the day to sneeze?

A Balanced Diet

Lisa Nicole Bell, author, filmmaker, entrepreneur, social change agent, and fellow Huntsvillian (from Huntsville, Alabama) diva designed a media pyramid which suggests an acceptable diet of information consumption. I love it because it's not strict like some nutritional diets that won't even let you look at a Popsicle. Lisa's diet lets you include things like "junk news" – as long as it's in small doses.

I would recommend this as a good starting point for anyone looking to find balance with all the information items available on the menu and, as social workers, there's a lot we could bombard ourselves with if we're not careful.

Lisa suggests that the bulk of a balanced information diet includes things that enrich like spiritual or personal development info, and that things like *Keeping Up With the Kardashians* (my guilty pleasure) only occupy three percent of one's consumption—the smallest part.

> *Physical obesity is not caused by the overload of available food; it is caused by the overcompensation of low-quality food. The same is true for mental obesity. – Darren Hardy*

Lisa Nicole Bell's Information Diet Pyramid

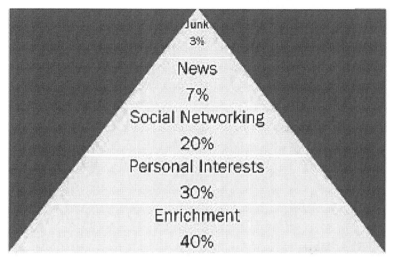

If you think about it, this is the perfect diet for a social worker or someone in the helping professions. It guarantees that, through personal and professional development, you ensure that you're continually improving as a person. Then, after you've filled yourself up, spend a great portion of your time educating yourself on things you love – your hobbies and personal interests – so automatically, 70% of your information diet is focused on you being the best *you* that you can be. How awesome is that!

Let me know if you come up with a better idea; until then, good luck and happy dieting.

Education is the ability to listen to almost anything without losing your temper or your self-confidence. — Robert Frost

Part 2: The Practice

Chapter 4

Operate in a Vacuum and Other Inefficiencies

If all the world were paper,

And all the sea were ink,

If all the trees

Were bread and cheese,

What should we have to drink?

~ Children's nursery rhyme

The Finer Things

I admit having a guilty pleasure: I love watching *Keeping Up With the Kardashians,* and if you don't know who the Kardashians are, you've either been hiding under a rock or haven't been born yet.

Don't get me wrong, I'm not so bad that I know the middle names of each character, or the sizes of their shoes, but what I like is to follow the adventures of this eccentric family, and plot a few of my own. There's something about all the fancy clothes and expensive homes that inspires me to want to experience some of those luxuries for myself, and believe that someday I will.

While I might not be able to afford the luxuries like VIP seating at the Grammys and NBA games, or the all-expense-paid trips to Dubai like the reality stars, as a social worker I also can't afford to throw temper tantrums when things don't go my way or call people outside of their names like "psycho", "bitch" or "man-whore".

In fact, there are several luxuries that social workers can't afford such as:

1. Operating in a vacuum

2. Taking human relationships for granted

3. Lack of integrity

4. Incompetence in practice

Of course there are more, but we'll stick to the short list.

Vacuums Suck

1. Operating in a Vacuum

For starters, the term 'vacuum' is synonymous with the words void, emptiness, space, nothingness, and blankness. When we say "operate in a vacuum" what we mean is that a thing is untouched by outside forces or is not influenced by external variables. It's what we say to express someone that does things on their own without regard for outside influences.

It's like that time when you were eight and your parents made you really angry and you wanted to say to them, "I don't need you! I don't need nobody!"

Okay, maybe that was just me.

But maybe you wanted to do your own thing and play by your own rules. Of course the truth was that you did need them, and eventually you even learned to appreciate them and work with the program they set.

Social Work Doesn't Do Vacuums

Social work, by nature of its craft, cannot exist in a vacuum. It's impossible. It's like asking a turtle to exist without its shell or a mirror to reflect something other than what's in front of it.

Impossible, right? Of course.

Ever seen one bee make honey from pollination to finished product or watched a loan beaver build a dam? Not regular things in the natural world. So why on earth do we highly intelligent and civilized mammals think we can do things on our own, without the input of others or regard for outside influences? Sure, we might be able to do some things, but ultimately we have to come together to accomplish any goal we set out to achieve. In reality, everything is being impacted and simultaneously impacting everything around it. It's universal law.

It really boils down to this: that all life is interrelated. We are all caught in an inescapable network of mutuality, tired into a single garment of destiny. Whatever affects one destiny, affects all indirectly. — Martin Luther King Jr.

Humankind has not woven the web of life. We are but one thread within it. Whatever we do to the web, we do to ourselves. All things are bound together. All things connect.— Chief Seattle

Systems Theory

In fact, one of the first things social work teaches is that we work with and within systems. Now, there's a whole theory about systems that we won't go into here, but suffice it to say that every thought, action, impulse, client, and agency is being impacted on, and is simultaneously impacting other thoughts, actions, impulses, clients, and agencies.

Crash

There's a great movie that I use to teach the profound impact of systems called *Crash* (2004). It highlights the often grave role that race, culture, impressions, prejudice, and beliefs have on our relationships, and how we influence and impact our environment just as much as it influences and impacts us.

For social workers this concept should be foremost at all times. It's what we use to help better contextualize the cases we encounter and provide workable approaches.

Ok, to catch you up on the movie in the event that you haven't seen the film, it follows several strangers whose lives "crash" into one another in various separate but interrelated events – generally antagonistically.

Every time I watch this movie I can't help but think how differently the situations could have turned out had the characters just taken the time to understand each other and their own triggers (and if you haven't seen it, you'll just have to watch it). Of course then I have to remind myself that it's only a movie, but the truth is, the scenarios it depicts happen all day every day in every corner of the world. The savvy social worker is aware that that this juicy mix of potentially volatile factors can create a smorgasbord of misunderstandings, inequality, and pain. The good news: it keeps life interesting. So it's to the professional's advantage to respect the interdependency of the systems they work with.

~ ~ ~

The smart social worker knows that it's the hidden systemic factors that lead to visible conditions.

~ ~ ~

For the People

2. Taking human relationships for granted

In the same vein, neither can social workers afford to take relationships (another systems element) for granted. How could we? I mean, that's our whole job!

Me, myself & I

Most of us (if we're normal) are selfish.

By selfish I mean that we view life from our own vantage point and are generally consumed in our own experiences. Sure, we consider others from time-to-time, but usually it's from a what's-in-it-for-me perspective.

To an extent, there's nothing wrong with being selfish. It makes sense that, as a helper, you're concerned about yourself enough to enable you to help others.

Take this book, for example. You're not reading it for me; you're reading it for you. Assuming you bathed this morning, even if your funk could repel the devil, chances are you didn't bathe to keep the devil away, but you wanted to be clean. This type of "selfishness" is actually necessary and productive and part of human functioning, so it's no problem.

The problem comes when we become so egotistical that we begin to take our relationships for granted.

There is no substitute for the comfort supplied by the utterly taken-for-granted relationship. — Iris Murdoch

But if you're a social worker, that's not even the worst part. The bigger tragedy comes when you fail to recognize the intricate and delicate interconnectedness of *every single relationship* that exists – the very foundation of our effectiveness if we are at all.

A man is called selfish not for pursuing his own good, but for neglecting his neighbor's.—Richard Whately

Just a final note about relationships in practice: chances are that most of our clients won't have the training and understanding about behavior and cognition that we do. This means the onus is on the social worker to ensure that the relationship remains professional and beneficial for the client.

I've seen card-carrying social workers lose their composure, and nearly their jobs because of a confrontation with a client.

What?!

If you're truly a professional social worker that should never happen. Now, I'm not saying that our clients can't behave disorderly and try our patience like Job, but I am saying that, as the trained professional, the social worker has got to be the bigger, more composed and competent person in the room.

And, yes, this *is* what you signed up for.

~ ~ ~

Professional social workers take responsibility for the quality of their relationships.

~ ~ ~

Integrity is Overrated

3. Lack of Integrity

If you're like me, I will bet you've never told a lie, or promised to do something that you never did do. I'll bet you never slack off on your responsibilities, and that you're always 100% committed to every task you undertake. I bet you're the picture of nobility in every ethical debate, and you probably give monthly to the Humane Society. (If you're *really* like me you'll know what a bunch o' bologna that is and that even in a perfect world...well, there is no perfect world now, is there?)

Let's be honest, we do slack off from time-to-time. We're human, aren't we? Humans slack off; humans can be biased, and they can be egotistical. But the social worker is Superhuman!

Yeah, right.

Okay, so we're not superhuman either. Let's at least agree that we're consistently conscientious and principal-based in our plans and actions. That qualifies as pretty exceptional, I think. When we're not, our results can show up looking something like this:

o Talking with no action

o Making empty promises

o Regularly letting others down

o Working at minimum standards

o Half-assing it

o Making a lot of noise

o Being in it to ~~win~~ lose it

So, the next thing social workers can't afford is lack of integrity in their work. It totally invalidates the whole point of the profession. It's like wearing a really nice outfit but forgetting to bathe (there goes that funk again); or having a lovely meal served for you on filthy dishes. One totally negates the other.

The *Oxford English Dictionary* (2005) defines integrity as the quality of being honest and morally upright. In social work this serves as the foundation for our ethical practice in the same way that our code of ethics serves as the foundation of our overall practice. As far as the social worker is concerned, our word is our bond and our talk is our walk.

Maintaining integrity for us is not a hassle or even an option, but a way of life.

Let me say that again.

Integrity for the social worker is a way of life. It's not just something we do from nine to five at our jobs, but it's a principle we adopt which not only governs our thoughts, but our words and actions as well. Social work puts such a premium on the practice of integrity that there are even sanctions for those that don't uphold it. Talk about your collateral expenses!

~~~

Professional social workers uphold their end of the proverbial stick.

~~~

Ignorance is Bliss

Tell the truth: you can probably name at least one person who you'd have no problem classifying as an idiot.

Oh, I know it's not politically correct – especially because I'm such a model social worker and all – but I'll bet as soon as you read that, the picture that popped in your head was of that nincompoop whose actions or ideas you've tried to rationalize or understand, but just can't. The truth is they're just ignorant. And I don't necessarily mean ignorant as in "dumb" as much as I mean "unaware" and their actions reflect this.

Of course! That's it. How else can you explain their otherwise unconsciousness and silly behavior? (I'm trying to be nice here.)

Well, social workers don't have this luxury either.

Nope. Not in our range of affordability. The real estate on incompetence is just too high.

Never ascribe to malice that which is adequately explained by incompetence – Napoleon Bonaparte

That smarts

4. Incompetence in practice

Let's qualify what we mean when we say "incompetence in practice."

Did you know that within the *Social Work Code of Ethics* (NASW and most other versions) is the principal of competence in practice?

Value: *Competence*

Ethical Principle: *Social workers practice within their areas of competence and develop and enhance their professional expertise.*

Social workers continually strive to increase their professional knowledge and skills and to apply them in practice. Social workers should aspire to contribute to the knowledge base of the profession.

I hope that speaks for itself. Anything less would be uncivilized.

Lesson Learned

So the idea is: say no to ignorance, educate yourself, and share the experiential wealth. This sure-fire formula will guarantee that the next time the idiot stick is being passed around, you can safely let it pass by you.

~ ~ ~

The smart social worker is a competent social worker.

~ ~ ~

Are you smarter than a 5th grader?

Real knowledge is to know the extent of one's ignorance.—Confucius

The highest form of ignorance is when you reject something you don't know anything about.—Wayne Dyer

Better to remain silent and be thought a fool than to speak and remove all doubt.—Abraham Lincoln

There is no darkness but ignorance.—William Shakespeare

I know nothing except the fact of my ignorance—Socrates

In a hierarchy, every employee tends to rise to his level of incompetence.—Laurence J. Peter

Nothing in the world is more dangerous than sincere ignorance and conscientious stupidity.—Martin Luther King, Jr.

Where ignorance is our master, there is no possibility of real peace.— Dalai Lama

Man cannot live by incompetence alone.—Charlotte Whitton

Never ascribe to malice that which is adequately explained by incompetence.—Napoleon Bonaparte

Ignorance; the root and stem of all evil.—Plato

It takes considerable knowledge just to realize the extent of your own ignorance—Thomas Sowell

Nothing is more terrible than to see ignorance in action.—Johann Wolfgang von Goethe

When ignorance gets started it knows no bounds.—Will Rogers

The recipe for perpetual ignorance is: Be satisfied with your opinions and content with your knowledge.—Elbert Hubbard

What We Know for Sure

We know for sure that social work is demanding in its execution – and I don't mean physically demanding as much as I mean ethically and emotionally demanding. It takes a lot of humility and strength (not to mention endurance) to work effectively with systems, manage relationships, maintain integrity, and remain competent in practice. Truthfully, sometimes we don't want to involve others in the decision-making process, and we don't feel like being respectful to some people, and it's not always easy to be the beacon of moral integrity, and God knows we've got enough on our plates to keep us busy without the challenge of continually striving to know more.

But we do have one luxury—one privilege—that keeps us all in balance and allows us to practice with integrity. We get to be fearless.

Fearless? Of course we are!

I think fear is what keeps us from going over the edge. I mean, as a race car driver, I don't think what makes a good race car driver is a fearless person. I think it's somebody that is comfortable being behind the wheel of something that's somewhat out of control.—Jeff Gordon

Let us not pray to be sheltered from dangers but to be fearless when facing them.—Rabindranath Tagore

Fate loves the fearless.—James Russell Lowell

The power of one, if fearless and focused, is formidable, but the power of many working together is better.—Gloria Macapagal Arroyo

It takes guts to stare in the face of incompetence and call its name. It takes bravery to put aside your own ego and show respect to the yelling client in your office. It takes courage to call your colleague out for bad practice, and it takes daring to continually pursue the path of justice even though your workload and paycheck say you can't afford to.

Who else but a bold, daring, fearless, person could do these?

If this sounds like a call to action, then so it is.

As social workers we don't have the luxury of sitting around on the sidelines complaining that things should be better. We're the unsung heroes – the ones who help to make things better. We don't have to stay incapacitated by some bogus no-it-can't-happen attitude. We're social workers, for cryin' out loud! Not some mamby pamby by the wayside weaklings walking around with our shoulders down and our hopes dashed against the rocks of despair.

We're social workers!

We're the advocates, the freedom fighters, the champions. We're the thinkers and the doers, the believers and the achievers, the big ballers and the shot callers, the Mamas and the Papas.

Wait. That was a band; but you get my drift.

So while we social workers might not ever be showcased on an episode of *Keeping Up With the Kardashians*, for us just knowing that when the shizzle hits the fan and people find themselves searching for direction in their lives, that our expertise is what's sought after and depended upon, makes our value priceless…and don't you forget it.

You are a box full of chocolates! —Khloe Kardashian

Chapter 5

Never, Ever Prepare Anything in Advance

Success depends upon previous-preparation, and without such-preparation-there is sure to be failure.
Confucius

What We Do

Social workers are called upon to do many things:

Public speaking
Grant and proposal writing
Individual counseling
Group counseling
Family counseling
Research and program development
Meeting with various stakeholders
Assessments, documentation and follow up
Home visits
Advocacy campaigns
Hospital visits
Policy development
School visits
Case conferences
Agency visits
Saving the world

In all of the tasks that social workers do there must be some amount of planning, even in the activity of saving the world.

~~~

The social worker who fails to plan, plans to fail.

~~~

Conspiracy Theory

So much of what social workers do is working with people who can be unpredictable. Luckily we have magic stuff called theory to give us frameworks for forecasting behaviors and situations. So theory helps us plan even when we're expecting the unexpected.

> *Plans are worthless, but planning is everything. There is a very great distinction because when you are planning for an emergency you must start with this one thing: the very definition of "emergency" is that it is unexpected, therefore it is not going to happen the way you are planning.—Dwight Eisenhower*

The virtue in planning is not so much the plan but in the process of planning. It's all about preparation for what may—or may not—occur.

What I Know for Sure

When it comes to planning for our work what I know for sure is that, even the best laid plans can go awry. So, the professional social worker has to have in her bag of tricks enough alternatives to seamlessly interchange them when the time comes. And trust me, it *will* come.

KW's story

> *I remember preparing a presentation for a group of girls who were wards of the state. The group session was to be about self-esteem as that was highlighted to be one of the major concerns among that population.*
>
> *When the session began and the girls heard the topic, they insisted and wanted to hear about sex, and how to get men and look more attractive to them. I insisted as I had only prepared to talk about self-esteem. Then I remembered that I had to meet the clients where they are. I quickly had to forget about my plan and divert to this topic in order to help these girls understand their sexuality and the importance of abstinence and the use of condoms. Also that a positive self-esteem will help them think highly of themselves and not look towards a man to make them feel complete.*
> *KW, Jamaica*

The Magic Key

I believe that the key to planning is to expect the unexpected. Inevitably, someone is going to be late; something is going to be forgotten; some document won't get signed; and the show will still go on. Even in the midst of the show, professional social workers who are flexible are the ones who succeed.

> *In fair weather, prepare for foul. – Thomas Fuller*

Where Planning Matters

If you happen to be a social worker in case management, then your planning is essentially with the client. Then there's social work administration that is almost entirely planning and monitoring of policies and programs. If we're doing any type of community or macro level work, planning is absolutely a given. And if you're the typical social worker, you may even have to plan your lunch breaks, or you run the risk of not eating at all.

While our social work literature spends plenty of time talking about planning for our clients, less is said about planning for ourselves as social work practitioners.

As you might have noticed by now, I'm a big advocate for personal wellness because, as I've said before, if you're not getting better for yourself, it's going to be nearly impossible to do better for your clients. Every good social worker I know has a self plan.

~ ~ ~

The smart social worker self plans for success.

~ ~ ~

Self Planning Defined

A self plan is the social worker's recognition that their personal wellness is critical to the social work process. Not only can the professional social worker *not* afford to *NOT* have one of these, but he or she recognizes that without one there's no way they can be effective long term. In fact, if you consider that structured within the social work process is the component of moving the client from dependence to independence (i.e. away from depending on you), you'll see this personal self planning stuff built right in.

Think about it: would you want your clients to depend on you forever? Of course not! Who wants to know that a year from now your client still needs your help to fill out an application for food stamps or facilitate their community meeting? That's why we stress the skill of empowerment, so they can do it themselves; and nothing says "I love me" more than an empowered client.

The A, B, C's of Self Planning

What are some things we can plan for ourselves that support this personal wellness? Here are a few suggestions to take into consideration:

1. Acknowledge your own worth
2. Begin to set boundaries
3. Celebrate your accomplishments
4. Do something fun
5. Empty your mind of stress
6. Follow your bliss
7. Garden
8. Hang out with positive people
9. Intend to enjoy each moment
10. Join a gym
11. Keep negative thoughts and people far away
12. Limit your contact with negative news
13. Meditate
14. Nap if you feel tired
15. Open a good book
16. Pray
17. Quiet your mind
18. Relax
19. Study information that inspires you
20. Take time to stop and smell the roses
21. Understand that self maintenance happens daily
22. Validate yourself; you're awesome!
23. Work smart, not hard
24. X-out the things that sap your energy
25. Yield to organization
26. Zone in to your spirit

Did you notice the alphabet theme? I made it up myself.

~ ~ ~

The smart social worker has an array of self-planning tricks to keep him/her in the game.

~ ~ ~

Personal Prep

I'll admit I'm not the most organized person in the world, which is why there is no better advocate for planning than I am. Plans help people like me accomplish things like eat lunch on a regular basis and finish this book. And in this modern world of technology, there are all kinds of planning tools that can be bought or downloaded for free from the internet to help you get organized and stay that way.

If planning to self plan seems a bit overwhelming, get some help. Hire a planner, or convince one of your really organized friends to assist. You don't have to do it alone, and, if you're anything like me, you probably can't.

If you don't design your own life plan, chances are you'll fall into someone else's plan. And guess what they have planned for you? Not much. — Jim Rohn

A good plan violently executed now is better than a perfect plan executed next week. — George S. Patton

You can never plan the future by the past. — Edmund Burke

Chapter 6

Don't Ask, Don't Tell, and Never Blow Any Whistles

Do what you feel in your heart to be right- for you'll be criticized anyway. You'll be damned if you do, and damned if you don't.—
Eleanor Roosevelt

Pat's Story

I was working as a young Community Social Worker, with a Government Agency in Jamaica.

On this beautiful afternoon my boss and I had to visit a community that needed power, running water and telephone services. We invited all the relevant agencies and the Member of Parliament to the meeting. Note that the community supported the opposing political party, of which the Member of Parliament did not belong.

The meeting was set in a community meeting area, and organized by an inexperienced Social Worker....not me, in a volatile community in Kingston, Jamaica.

We arrived at the meeting greeted by two (2) armed police officers seated in the vehicle, as they were fearful of leaving their jeep. We were greeted by the Social Worker, who assured us that everything was ok, and ready to go.

We started the meeting on time, with presentations on the way, but I noted with care that the meeting was attended by only women, not one man from the community was present. A few minutes into the proceedings, I noticed that a group of young men were walking

*towards the community meeting room with really tall guns, in plain
sight.*

*I had no idea of what was about to happen, nor what I should
d...it wasn't in a book. I looked onto my colleagues who were
standing close by, and they saw what was happening. The young
men got to the door and asked in a loud and intimidating voice
"what is going on here?" The Social Worker attempted to respond
to the young men about the meeting and its purpose. When they
heard that residents wanted telephones, they became angry, and
started calling the women present "informers". As the angry mob
continued to vent their anger, I just stepped in, and asked if I may
explain, they said "go ahead, let's hear you". I then turned to the
men and the women, referred to them as mothers and fathers and
explained how having the services would assist their children, and
their community.*

*The women soon became angry with the young men, and chased
them away, said they wanted better for their children, and they
wanted us to stay. The young men turned and left the meeting.*

*I have come to learn that being older is not always wiser, and
certainly working as a team in any situation is crucial for the bet-
terment of our clients.*

Patrice Samuels, Kingston, Jamaica


~~~
*Sometimes the professional social worker has to be
braver than most.*
~~~


Myrna's Story

*I had responsibility for a recently funded therapeutic foster care
program and a seasoned clinical social worker was assigned to the
project, having been selected by top management.*

*A requirement was weekly home visits where in-home teaching,
checking facilities, assessing the child's progress and dealing with the
foster parent's concerns/issues etc. were expected.*

*On one visit I decided to accompany the worker to model good
practice and to get a first had glimpse for myself.*

Tom had recently been adopted so was no longer a foster child and the assumption was that he no longer fell under the agency's jurisdiction. All seemed fine on the surface until I asked where the child slept; I had not noted a bed for him. There was a lot of fumbling and an explanation that he loves to sleep on the floor.

"That's fine but where is his bed?" The explanation was that it was in the shed.

After being given a day to get the bed from the shed there was still no bed because, as I suspected, there was no bed!

How could a "seasoned" clinical social worker have missed this for nearly a year? What message of displacement was sent to this newly adopted child, a child who had been abandoned and neglected?

The moral of this story is that length of time in the field does not spell competence and honesty and integrity should not be taken for granted. Had this worker been diligent and thorough? Had she actually been visiting? These are all questions that were raised as a result of that incident. On the surface this may seem like a minor incident, but the trauma of foster care does not need the help of our professionals to further damage our children.

Myrna Baily, Washington DC

~~~

Professional social workers are keen observers.

~~~

Confrontation Appreciation

Every social worker has heard about whistle blowing or the social work role of initiator. This is a very fundamental role of social work as the initiator calls attention to an issue or problem.

"If you can't advocate for yourself how are you going to expect to advocate for your clients?" I heard this phrase repeated over and over throughout my college experience from my professors. I'll admit it took me a while to grasp this lesson internally, though. I'm a natural born rebel – strong willed I've been told. As a bit of self disclosure, I was raised in a family where displays of strong will

were regarded as disrespectful, and a thing to be disciplined out of you and molded into respect (i.e. don't talk back, do as you're told, and don't question authority – all anti social work advocacy strategies). This learned helplessness manifested itself in various forms in my work and relationships. At one point after a colleague and I had been treated unfairly by our directors she exclaimed in frustration, "Don't you ever fight back? My God, get a backbone!"

Even in the face of injustice I wasn't always comfortable with speaking up. I've had to learn to appreciate the activity of confrontation, and it's come through (would you believe?) the activity of confrontation.

New York on My Mind

One of my first and most memorable confrontational experiences came on a bus in New York. I was standing in a packed isle and a woman came on the bus with about six or seven young children. They looked like stair steps ranging in ages of about three to nine.

Well, she started yelling and cursing at the children to sit down and shut up. She even slapped the youngest one who was fidgeting in her seat presumably trying to get comfortable.

My fellow passengers were obviously disturbed with the woman's verbal and physical outbursts and gasped when she raised her hand to hit the small child, now crying, yet again.

In the most commanding, bellowing voice I could muster I said, "Lady, I'm a social worker and if you hit that child one more time I will call social services so fast your head will spin."

There's so much more I wanted to say and probably more I could have done, but considering it was my first public confrontation, I was shaking and nervous. I didn't know if she was going to turn around and threaten me or punch me or what. Instead she just froze.

Some of the other passengers made grumblings of support, and I swear I saw gratitude in the eyes of two children in her care that bravely looked up to see the face of the woman who dared to challenge their tormentor's authority.

Even though her back was facing me she must have felt my eyes burning holes into the back of her head because she hurriedly got off at the next stop.

That was the first time I felt the power of my profession first hand – "Lady, I'm a social worker" – and I've been riding it ever since.

Advocacy First Hand

When I was teaching social work at a university one of my students relayed to me an incident about a neglected child in the hospital in Jamaica.

Now, Jamaica is a beautiful place, but still has a way to go as far as 'respect for the dignity and worth of the person' is concerned across all sectors.

This student, upon observing an infant left unattended and crying hysterically by nursing staff, called to the attention of the staff that the child obviously needed some consideration. Knowing the probable and sure-enough reaction of the annoyed nurses, she confronted the blatant disregard for the child's right to care and protection and called their butts on it. This kind of whistle blowing is what separates the helper from the helpless, the advocate from the advisory, and the social worker from the social bystander.

Never be afraid to raise your voice for honesty and truth and compassion against injustice and lying and greed. If people all over the world...would do this, it would change the earth. — *William Faulkner*

What It Is

What we're really talking about here is advocacy. It's a trademark role of the social work profession. But advocacy can take on different forms. Sometimes it looks like offering support for a government bill. Other times it may look like attacking propaganda. The true advocate, unlike the chapter's title, asks lots of questions, speaks truth to power, and blows many whistles; and that, boys and girls, is the first step to change.

One can find many examples in society of an advocate: Mother Theresa advocated for the poor, Dr. Martin Luther King, Jr. advocated for civil rights for blacks, and Neo advocated for a world free from machine control (it's a Matrix thing). As long as there is inequality there will be advocates in the world. And if you subscribe to conflict theory, then a conflict is inevitable.

Mind you, I'm not saying there aren't such things as advocacy mishaps – times when a good cause falls prey to bad practice; happens to the best of us from time to time. So as a way to stave off these threats of poor performance, I offer the following safeguards to help us all follow best practice in our endeavors.

Advocacy Fab 5

1. **Don't avoid problems, confront them.** This could be as simple as a conversation (and usually is) or as entailed as a campaign for world peace. Whatever the issue that sparks your fire, don't avoid it, confront it, especially if someone else is at risk of harm if you don't.

2. **Choose your battles.** I believe it is possible to live a consciously balanced life without getting overwhelmed. If you're called to this profession there will be no shortage of problems that grab your attention. Which ones are you going to take on? You can't save the whole world, but you can help to save the environment, or a child

from abuse or a community center from being turned into a parking lot. It's your choice. Choose wisely.

3. **Don't abandon your standards of practice.** If you see something, say something. If you feel that blowing the whistle or confrontation may be at a risk to your personal safety, seek confidential support in how to proceed.

4. **Don't assume a position of intimidation.** This is not the same thing as "Don't assume a position of humility." Those are two separate positions and humility is often well received. The ego can be a formidable contender and most people don't like to be corrected. If there's a cause you believe in, by all means, stand up for it, but do your best to find tactful ways to confront situations. If you, however, buy into an inferior position of intimidation, especially when you've got policy on your side, you set a precedent that social work is weak, and it's not – it's power!

5. **Check yourself before you wreck yourself.** If you recognize you've become indifferent, annoyed, neglectful, or blatantly disrespectful to issues you once cared about, check yourself, and by that I mean stop and assess what's going on for you (and it's *always* about you – how you choose to react) before your oblivion does any significant damage to your clients or your cause.

I'm passionate about people. I've spent my life in advocacy. People matter - whether or not we agree on the issue, people matter. – Ann Marie Buerkle

Chapter 7

Bare Your Bias

What are little girls made of? (2X)
Sugar and spice and all that's nice,
That's what little girls are made of.

What are little boys made of? (2x)
Frogs and snails and puppy dog tails,
That's what little boys are made of.
—Nursery rhyme

Bias? What Bias?

"Anyone who thinks that there is bias in this world is crazy; of course I can say that because I'm so smart.

Furthermore, anyone who thinks that there is no gender bias is probably a man because everyone knows women are always the ones getting the short end of the stick."

It's part of our human experience to be biased in some things, right? I mean, if I have a baby it's, of course, the most beautiful baby in the world, and there's no better profession than social work, am I wrong? The truth is there are all sorts of bias out there and it's impossible to avoid it in every instance.

The way to Heaven is ascending; we must be content to travel up-hill, though it be hard and tiresome, and contrary to the natural bias of our flesh.– Jonathan Edwards

When we talk about bias we're really talking about the elements of prejudice, preconceived ideas, and partiality. Usually these are easy to spot because they show up as some form of 'ism': sexism, racism, ageism, etc. Someone who operates from a biased perspective can never be fair. It's counterintuitive to the biased nature. And considering social work's whole focus is on equality and social justice, these influences have no place in its camp.

Jackie's Story

While working with a self-proclaimed Christian social worker with responsibility to address the needs of court appointees, a young woman came into the probation office to seek information and support about her partner's court case. Though she was polite enough, her piercings and tattoos obviously threw my colleague off because as soon as she asked a question about the case, my colleague began lecturing her on how inappropriate her dress was and how her partner, obviously, was the type of person who deserved whatever sentence the judge handed down.

I was so embarrassed for my colleague, but because she is senior to me, I couldn't say anything at that point in front of her. The client was visibly upset but tried to remain polite. As she left I pulled her aside and apologized to her for my colleague's behavior, but I haven't seen her since.
Jackie H., Mandeville Jamaica

~ ~ ~

The professional social worker uses critical judgment
with parking spaces, not with people.

~ ~ ~

What's Your Bias?

Let's face it, we're influenced by our environments. For those raised in traditional Christian homes, things like homosexuality and sex outside of marriage are probably taboo. And for the conservative elite, things like piercings and tattoos might be offensive fashion. Whatever your bias may be, the key is to know its name, call it out, and never let it show its ugly face in your professional social work practice.

Be curious, not judgmental. – Walt Whitman

UPR

In case it seems impossible to function completely free from bias, prejudice, and with no prejudgment whatsoever, Carl Rogers came up with a guaranteed way to ensure that, even if we do have these thoughts, our clients will never be the wiser. He termed it 'unconditional positive regard' and it's the practice of showing our clients and colleagues respect no matter what they look like, how they behave, what they may say, how they may say it, and especially how we may personally feel about them.

Unconditional positive regard helps to ensure that our clients feel accepted (or at least not judged) by us which, in turn, helps to build trust – the magic ingredient in the helping process.

The Acid Test

You might remember the WWJD (What Would Jesus Do?) campaign that was popular in the early 1990's. People sported WWJD wristbands, WWJD caps, and WWJD T-shirts. I saw so many WWJD bumper stickers I started to imagine that maybe Jesus would rather walk than drive with those stickers all over His car!

At any rate, the campaign was an international success, selling over 15,000,000 wristbands alone in 1997 and challenging people from all walks of life to stop, even if just for a second, and consider if the choices they were making in each moment were choices that Jesus himself would make.

Powerful stuff.

The success of this simple campaign proved that we human beings have within us the power to choose our thoughts, words and deeds in every moment of our existence. We'll never know how many arguments were averted, crimes were prevented, or teenage hormones subdued because people decided to consider the perspective of a higher calling.

And if we have the power to choose these things, we can always choose the opinion, the comment or the action that's free from prejudice, bias, or otherwise harmful judgment of our clients as well.

The Fourth Law

In Deepak Chopra's book entitled *The Seven Laws of Spiritual Success* (1994), he outlines seven principles which he says are fundamental to real success in our lives. Relevant to our discussion here is his fourth suggested principle, the "Law of Least Effort." This is the principle of harmony and love, and below is his mantra for applying this law.

APPLYING THE LAW OF LEAST EFFORT

I will put the Law of Least Effort into effect by making a commitment to take the following steps:

(1) I will practice Acceptance. Today I will accept people, situations, circumstances, and events as they occur. I will know that this moment is as it should be, because the whole universe is as it should be. I will not struggle against the whole universe by struggling against this moment. My acceptance is total and complete. I accept things as they are this moment, not as I wish they were.

(2) Having accepted things as they are, I will take Responsibility for my situation and for all those events I see as problems. I know that taking responsibility means not blaming anyone or anything for my situation (and this includes myself). I also know that every problem is an opportunity in disguise, and this alertness to opportunities allows me to take this moment and transform it into a greater benefit.

(3) Today my awareness will remain established in Defenselessness. I will relinquish the need to defend my point of view. I will feel no need to convince or persuade others to accept my point of view. I will remain open to all points of view and not be rigidly attached to any one of them.

The heart of the matter

If we look deeply enough at ourselves we may discover that every inclination toward bias, prejudice, favoritism, partiality, and discrimination has its roots in our own insecurities and unwillingness to accept as they are the people, situations, circumstances and events we encounter. It's a habit of perception we've picked up from our surroundings and, if left unchecked, has the makings of destruction and harm for our clients within it.

But the smart social worker, the conscientious social worker, the introspective social worker whose aim it is to grow, and the mature social worker knows that nothing's ever about the client until its first about the self; and once the self is in check, the client is in good hands to get help.

An open mind keeps all its doors and windows closed for fear, worry, anxiety, hate, selfishness, jealousy and bias nature. – Anuj Somany

Chapter 8

Believe Everything You Hear

Courage is what it takes to stand up and speak; courage is also what it takes to sit down and listen. — Winston Churchill

The Hear

Social work uses scientific-empirical data to help substantiate our observations and otherwise generic assessments (that's social work-speak for we backup our theories with facts).

In order to understand a person and their situation, social workers study and assess things like the person's environment and their level of functioning. And in order to do this, the professional social worker must hear.

When I say "hear" I'm not just talking about the ability to perceive sound. I'm talking about the skill of listening; the ability to pay attention to what is being said by the communicator even if no words are used at all.

Social workers who perform at the highest levels practice listening as a skill vital to their success, and it makes sense; how else can we understand our clients and other stakeholders if we don't truly listen to them and hear what they are communicating?

The Wise Ones Speak

Consider the following quotes about listening. If possible, see if you can "hear" what the author was intending to convey. Write down your thoughts and compare with a partner. You may even be inspired to pen your own.

There are people who, instead of listening to what is being said to them, are already listening to what they are going to say themselves.—Albert Guinon

The first duty of love is to listen.—Paul Tillich

A good listener is not only popular everywhere, but after a while he gets to know something.—Wilson Mizner

It takes two to speak the truth - one to speak and another to hear.—Henry David Thoreau

A good listener is not someone with nothing to say. A good listener is a good talker with a sore throat.—Katharine Whitehorn

Make sure you have finished speaking before your audience has finished listening.—Dorothy Sarnoff

The best time to hold your tongue is the time you feel you must say something or bust.—Josh Billings

Listen or thy tongue will keep thee deaf.—Native American

Man who know little say much. Man who know much say little.—Author Unknown

It is the province of knowledge to speak and it is the privilege of wisdom to listen.—Oliver Wendell Holmes

To listen closely and reply well is the highest perfection we are able to attain in the art of conversation.—Francois de La Rochefoucauld

Be a good listener. Your ears will never get you in trouble.—*Frank Tyger*

Listen. Do not have an opinion while you listen because frankly, your opinion doesn't hold much water outside of Your Universe. Just listen. Listen until their brain has been twisted like a dripping towel and what they have to say is all over the floor.—*Hugh Elliott*

There is no such thing as a worthless conversation, provided you know what to listen for. And questions are the breath of life for a conversation.—*James Nathan Miller*

Know how to listen, and you will profit even from those who talk badly.—*Plutarch*

As I get older, I've learned to listen to people rather than accuse them of things.—*Po Bronson*

Listen. Don't explain or justify.—*William G. Dyer*

Nature gave us one tongue and two ears so we could hear twice as much as we speak.—*Epictetus*

From listening comes wisdom, and from speaking repentance.—*Italian Proverb*

The greatest gift you can give another is the purity of your attention.—*Richard Moss*

Every person I work with knows something better than me. My job is to listen long enough to find it and use it.—*Jack Nichols*

It is only by closing the ears of the soul, or by listening too intently to the clamors of the sense, that we become oblivious of their utterances.—*Alexander Crummell*

Wisdom is the reward for a lifetime of listening ... when you'd have preferred to talk. – D.J. Kaufman

Much silence makes a powerful noise.—African Proverb

The greatest compliment that was ever paid me was when one asked me what I thought, and attended to my answer.—Henry David Thoreau

The hearing ear is always found close to the speaking tongue.— Ralph Waldo Emerson

A good listener tries to understand what the other person is saying. In the end he may disagree sharply, but because he disagrees, he wants to know exactly what it is he is disagreeing with.—Kenneth A. Wells

Listening is an attitude of the heart, a genuine desire to be with another which both attracts and heals.—J. Isham

Better to remain silent and be thought a fool than to speak out and remove all doubt. —Abraham Lincoln

The 5th Habit

Inherent in those last pages of script was the integral point of listening to another's point of view. Author Stephen Covey also suggests that the number five habit of highly effective people is that they seek *first* to understand, *then* to be understood.

I have to say, I've seen this principle in action and it works. The number one desire of any person, he suggests, is to be understood, and it's true.

If you ever want to get your point across to someone, Covey advises that you first listen attentively to what the other person is saying, repeat it to them so that they get the sense that you were really paying attention, affirm their feelings, and *then* relay your position. In general, if this is done successfully, the person will feel understood by you and you're more likely to win their respect, their regard and their cooperation.

When you really listen to another person from their point of view, and reflect back to them that understanding, it's like giving them emotional oxygen. —*Stephen Covey*

Stacy-Ann's Story

As an example of how NOT to practice social work as it relates to listening, read Stacy-Ann's story below.

Each time a client shares a story with me I tend to want to finish it for them.

One day while counseling a new client she became annoyed by my constant interruptions and shouted, "Shut up; won't you let me finish?!" I just froze and stared.

~ ~ ~

Good social workers know to have their ears open more than their mouths are.

~ ~ ~

Listen With Your Eyes

Most of us have read the statistics which report that much of our communication is actually non-verbal. Depending on your data source this could be as much as 94%. The rest is divided into verbal indicators of what is said and the tone in which it is delivered, but the majority is said to be through our bodies.

You would have had firsthand experience of contradictory messages yourself; someone flatters you while rolling their eyes, or wishes you a good day with an aggressive tone. Perhaps you've been the one on the disingenuous side of the table, grieving with your eyes while smiling with your lips, or using no words at all to convey your impatience save a nervous shake of the leg.

For the social worker to really be effective, she will have to enlist the superpowers of discernment and sensitivity to snuff out the underlying truth in her encounters. I'm not claiming this to be an easy feat, but the caution is to be alert to, not only what our clients tell us, but to their nonverbal actions as well.

A Learning Experience

I once had a client named John (not his real name, of course). Now, John had me fooled – or I was a fool – whichever way you want to look at it. But he had me believing that he was the nicest, sweetest, most innocent reformed ex-con drug user/physical abuser on the planet. I later found out that, not only was he a pathological liar, but I had a lot to learn about what it took to really listen to my clients.

If I didn't notice the bruises on his hands, I should have picked up the alcohol on his breath, or inquired further about his repeated absence from our appointments. I should have probed when he denied having an altercation with his partner, instead of assuming that his cautioned tone was merely him taking time to think.

But I was young and inexperienced, or so I'd like to believe. So when his girlfriend came looking for me, crying to me, showing me her bruises and recounting how he had repeatedly battered and raped her, you could have scraped me off the floor with a shovel; I was gobsmacked (that's British slang for verklempt which is Yiddish for floored which is English slang for being stunned with emotion).

See, to her it didn't matter that her partner and I had good rapport, or that I had a degree from an Ivy League school. It didn't matter that I was young or naïve, and it certainly didn't matter that my impression of him was that of a reformed abuser. What mattered to her was that I had missed the signs, and she as a result, had suffered the consequences.

A Call to Honesty

If social work does nothing else, it calls us to be brave, to be courageous, and to be honest with ourselves and with our clients. Allegiance to its cause demands that we pay attention to the nuances and idiosyncrasies of the individuals and arenas with which we work. I suppose part of social work's dharma is to teach us to apply the patience and perseverance it takes to develop the skills of honest listening. When we do this we not only connect to the true message of the individual or cause, but we begin a ripple effect of true healing for our clients as well as their circles of influence, and sometimes for ourselves.

And if that's not what social work's about, then what is it?

Effective listeners remember that "words have no meaning - people have meaning." The assignment of meaning to a term is an internal process; meaning comes from inside us. And although our experiences, knowledge and attitudes differ, we often misinterpret each other's messages while under the illusion that a common understanding has been achieved. — Larry Barker

Chapter 9

Don't Change a Single Person, Place or Thing

My Father had a profound influence on me. He was a lunatic.
— Spike Milligan

She Said *WHAT*?!

I couldn't believe what I had just heard. Even though my student had informed me that her on-site supervisor had actually discouraged her from seeking out clients to help, I was actually hearing it now with my own ears.

Let me give some background information.

Social work is, for the most part, a practice-based profession. So it's essential that social workers get a chance to actually practice and apply the theory they learn in the classroom or else how can social work be legitimized as a real skill?

One particular student, we'll call her Carrie, had an interest in social work within the medical system, so she was placed within a hospital – an ideal placement for clinical practice – except that the student complained about not having any work to do.

No work to do? In a hospital? How could that be?

"We don't look for work for ourselves," her supervisor told me. "We just wait until someone calls us for something. If they need something they'll find us. Until then, she (our student) can read or play-Solitaire."

~ ~ ~

The professional social worker chooses proactively over reactivity every day.

~ ~ ~

Lie to Me

My student was right. I had tried to encourage her to stick it out, use her initiative, approach her this way instead of that way, but none of it seemed to work, and now I knew why. It wasn't my student's fault that she wasn't seeing clients with laundry lists of problems; she had done all she could.

Nope. It wasn't her. It was her on-site supervisor; the one with the Its-not-my-problem attitude and a lackluster approach to anything that happened before 5 p.m. How, I wondered, could a social worker not be busy, and in a public hospital? I had heard the answer, but was in such disbelief that all I could do was repeatedly ask the rhetorical question in my head.

She said *WHAT*?!

It was as if my mind wouldn't allow me to comprehend such blatant disregard from a colleague—a social worker!

She said *WHAT*?!

And with that, my student was promptly removed and relocated to a more proactive facility.

Don't try to win over the haters; you are not a jackass whisperer.
— Brené Brown

~ ~ ~

Professional Social Workers know that the difference between action and inaction is indifference.

~ ~ ~

Indifference

Indifference may be the single most dangerous threat to the advancement and respect of professional social work. It flies in the face of all things social work and the would-be social worker that harbors indifference should go back to step one – self analysis.

INDIFFERENCE; It takes 43 muscles to frown and 17 to smile, but it doesn't take any to just sit there with a dumb look on your face (Despair.com).

Resources

I remember being a young social worker and just starting out on my career journey. What would I see? Who would I meet? And when in the world was I going to be able to remember all those theories?

It never occurred to me at the time, that while I was waiting to catch up to my profession, my profession was waiting to hear from me.

But who was I and what did I know? And what could I possibly offer my profession?

Bloom Where You are Planted

I once heard a graduation speech that resonated with me as much then as it does now. The focus of the speaker's message was "bloom where you are planted." In essence, his message to the graduating class was that you may not always land the dream job or be in the position you'd like to be in, but do your best with the opportunities presented to you and, in due course, you're sure to be rewarded for your efforts.

Social workers, too, have a responsibility to bloom where they are planted. But let's take it a step further; we must also do some planting. A fellow colleague and I used to challenge our students on Field Placement to "leave a legacy."

The Writing is on the Wall

If you were a typical teenager it's probable that you wrote your name on some bathroom wall or carved it on some old oak tree, "So-and-so was here." It's a rite of passage, a tradition of sorts. It's a way to leave your mark on the world and to show the universe that you exist.

Well, just as indelible as those marks on that tree, social workers leave their marks on the lives and experiences of the clients they serve. Again, this goes back to our previous discussion on making sure that we listen to our clients and do no harm, as our influence is endless.

Think twice before you speak, because your words and influence will plant the seed of either success or failure in the mind of another. Napoleon Hill

But every encounter, every conversation, and every interaction is an opportunity for the social worker to leave a mark, and impressions can be fragile things.

While it may be impossible to control how your client interprets your words and actions, it's entirely possible to contribute to the profession in more tangible ways. This book, for example, is a seed deliberately planted. You might improve the service delivery system at your agency or modify a resource manual. You might conduct and publish research that helps to inform another's practice, or simply sign a petition that leads to improved access to care. The idea is to leave a place better off because you were there.

Whatever your state is, bloom where you are planted, and plant where you are placed. Unfortunately my colleague did neither bloom nor plant and her practice suffered as a result of it.

~ ~ ~

Trained Social Work Professionals know the monumental significance of leaving a place better off than we encountered it.

~ ~ ~

Perhaps you've read the following quote by Marion Williamson from her book *A Return to Love* (1992). It's one of my favorites and one that I think can be especially meaningful for social work practice. Consider it now in the context of our discussion on conscious impact and ask yourself the question, am I practicing in a way that honors my true self and makes a difference in the world? If your answer is no, it's never too late to start.

> *Our deepest fear is not that we are inadequate. Our deepest fear is that we are powerful beyond measure. It is our light, not our darkness that most frightens us. We ask ourselves, Who am I to be brilliant, gorgeous, talented, fabulous? Actually, who are you not to be? You are a child of God. Your playing small does not serve the world. There is nothing enlightened about shrinking so that other people won't feel insecure around you. We are all meant to shine, as children do. We were born to make manifest the glory of God that is within us. It's not just in some of us; it's in everyone. And as we let our own light shine, we unconsciously give other people permission to do the same. As we are liberated from our own fear, our presence automatically liberates others.*

Part 3: The Profession

Chapter 10

Don't Qualify Yourself

At one time I thought he wanted to be an actor. He had certain qualifications, including no money and a total lack of responsibility. – Hedda Hopper

Let's Start With a Riddle

Riddle me this:

Suzy has been working in a social work-related post for more than 6 years but has never received social work specific training. Is she a social worker?

    a. Yes
    b. No
    c. It depends
    d. Jury's still out

If you've been trained as a professional social worker you've likely had the "how-dare-they-call-themselves-social-workers" discussion with members of your program. More than likely this conversation came up when someone was retelling an encounter they had had with a self-proclaimed "social worker" who was doing something very…"un-social worky." Or maybe it came during a debate about the use of the term "Social Worker" in a job title with qualifications similar to, but not entirely social work.

Maybe the argument got heated when it was mentioned that many non-social work degree holding professionals used the title of "social worker" whenever it seemed convenient, and perhaps you discussed that it was often used whenever holidays or natural disasters came around – then everyone who handed out a canned item or knit scarf was a social worker.

So, back to the million-dollar question: is Suzy a social worker or not?

Conundrum, Anyone?

Let's consider the following:

1. A lot of what social workers do, other people do too
Let's be honest: social workers perform many of the same tasks as people in other professions. Heck, as people in general! Take, for example, the principle of respect. I mean, social workers are big on respect.

Respect?

You would expect that to be a given for every human being just by virtue of existing on the planet. But, no. Social workers make it a point to highlight this principle and talk about it every chance they get.

Not to mention they're very helpful (…obviously. It's a helping profession, after all). They listen without showing bias, empathize with their clients, and are proactive problem solvers. Maybe that's why so many people don't take social workers seriously – they think they're just being polite.

Keeping other people's business to themselves is another one, except they call it being confidential. I knew a lady whom I could tell anything to. She was very confidential, but I would always have to remind her of our conversations…on second thought, maybe she was just forgetful.

2. *As the profession evolves, the profession expands*
Have you ever had an idea in your mind about something you wanted to create – maybe it was a drawing or a meal, a business or a melody – only to find that, when you'd finished, it wasn't quite what you had in mind to begin with, but you still liked it? Well, that's kind of what I'm talking about.

While a recognized amalgamation of psychology, sociology, spirituality and science, the profession itself has, in recent years, birthed several offspring related to specific aspects of its function (i.e. Human Services). This means that there are more things to know as a social worker; and rightly so. With the growing complexity of human circumstances and characteristics, it makes sense to seek specialized skill sets to meet those unique needs.

So, the profession is ever morphing. I wonder if Suzy is aware of that.

Two Choices

Human Services, Social Care, Social Entrepreneurialism, and other branches of Social Work have risen to give voice to special facets of the profession, claiming right in their own specialty and finding distinction in contrast to traditional social work practices. So, even though we may qualify ourselves with a first or second or third degree, our profession continues to expand.

We can look at these changes in two ways: fight the distinctions or support the variety. However your boat floats, we can all agree that every aspect of our work holds value. I mean sure, a kayak can float, but would you book it for your honeymoon cruise? I doubt it. You'd want the vessel that's made specifically for cruising, not the one whose value is lost on the misuse of its purpose. In like manner, wouldn't you want to utilize the services of the social worker that most appropriately meet your needs? Of course you would.

So, what about Suzy?

The Point Is...

While I'm not sure if I'm doing a good job, my attempt is to highlight the need for training and some sort of qualification in the field, otherwise you'll be flying by the seat of your pink hot pants in the middle of winter, and in the world of social work that's called reckless endangerment (and sometimes it's called a lawsuit).

I once wrote about this very topic while at Northern Caribbean University as the head of the Social Work Program. The article entitled "Not Everyone is a Social Worker" was published in the *Jamaica Gleaner*, August 2009. At the risk of boring you further, just read it already!

NOT EVERYONE IS A SOCIAL WORKER

At its recently held annual commencement ceremony, Northern Caribbean University (NCU) graduated 56 persons from the Social Work Program out of the Department of Behavioral Sciences, with a dozen more graduating in absentia. In only its second graduation cycle the program boasted the largest make up of Behavioral Sciences participants surpassing Counseling, Guidance Counseling, and Psychology sectors in the department.

THE TREND

In the last three years, the number of persons enrolling in social work programs has significantly increased on the island. What this says to me is that there is a growing demand for professional training within the field of social intervention. It also speaks to the immediate need that exists for these interventions to be implemented in Jamaican society.

THE FIELD

Social work has been an elusive concept around the world for decades, mainly because of its abstract nature and definition. In Jamaica there is a rich and commendable history of individuals and social activist groups which have worked effectively to impact positive change through hands-on intervention. In essence, social work shares many of the same skills and values that have made these noble accomplishments possible. Today, however, social work as a profession is much more than mere helping alone.

Throughout its development, social workers have persevered tirelessly to qualify the profession of social work as a science through research and practice. It becomes a point of contention, then, for some who would call themselves social workers without the formal and internationally recognized indoctrination of knowledge, values and skills to legitimize the training.

In short, social work is the professional service of helping through intervention. It entails involvement with all sectors of society including individuals, families, groups, organizations and communities. To do this effectively, the social work practitioner must consider areas of biological, psychological, social and spiritual development, and network with many different stakeholders in the process. While the social worker is trained in areas of counseling and psychological development, he or she is not bound to work in any static situation, but generally works within and across sectors to empower clients to reach their optimal levels of development. Traditionally, social workers are found working in agencies that provide direct social services such as the Victim Support Unit, Hospitals, the Child Development Agency and the Probation Office. However, they can also be found in places like schools, financial institutions, and at the highest levels of government developing policies that positively impact the society and, because of their first hand knowledge of issues, quite arguably, may be the best candidates to do so.

THE CONFLICT

While it is true that trained social workers are suited to function in many different roles and under many different titles, the profession does not endorse a reciprocal approach to accept persons, not having had years of academic training as social workers, to assume the title unto themselves.

The title of Social Worker is a designation reserved for those who have been professionally trained and have practiced within the field. You wouldn't make the mistake of calling a nurse a doctor just because they perform many of the same functions, or someone who plants a flower a florist just because they both deal with plants. Likewise, the trained social worker is a specialist within his field and has been tested and accepted at the academic and practice levels. The line is precariously drawn, then, when speaking to those without the formal training who for years have referred to and thought of themselves as social workers. Though an uncomfortable distinction to make for all involved, in order to ensure quality control and accountability maintenance, professional social workers make no apology for this. Now, more than ever, is the best time to highlight this peculiarity.

THE PLAN

Jamaica is ripe for professional social workers as more focus is being given to the systematic implementation of workable solutions to historical issues such as sexual abuse, domestic violence, police corruption, illiteracy, teenage pregnancy, deportees, HIV/AIDS, and the mentally ill. Right now we have the best opportunity to capitalize on the skills of social workers to work in schools, clinics, children's homes, nursing homes, and even prisons. In fact, in order for Jamaica to move forward with its plans to reach developed country status, all sectors of Jamaican society must heavily incorporate these professionals within the capacity of what's working currently, and use them to further assist in finding successful solutions.

There are no easy answers to Jamaicans' social problems, but by incorporating trained social workers like those who have just completed studies at NCU, Jamaica can confidently expect to improve its social situation. I congratulate the recent graduates and challenge all professionally trained social workers in every sector to model, practice and promote the knowledge, values and skills that make social work the noble profession that it is. We are counting on you to make professional social work matter.

Do you think you're ready to answer that riddle yet?

The importance of qualification

As you may have gathered, social workers make a big deal about becoming qualified – that is, going through training and a certification process that legitimizes one's work, and this qualification serves several purposes.

Let's face it. We live in a society that rewards "achievers," and a widely considered achievement all over the world today is having letters behind your name—you know, the Esq., Ed.D., MSW, or PhD. Though this perspective is changing – and my personal definition of success marks achievement less by scholastic accomplishment and more by following one's passion and joy (which may not require the person to even attain a high school diploma) – for social work, the professional exposure has its own advantages.

5 Advantages (For Now) For Getting a Higher Education in Social Work or Its Related Fields

1. Advantage #1: It gives you a greater platform from which to advocate influentially (People will listen to you more readily).

2. Advantage #2: Qualification helps to fill in the gaps in a knowledge base where experience is not enough (You can't experience everything; some things have to be understood first).

3. Advantage #3: You're likely to make more money as a professionally trained helper than as an untrained one (Makes sense).

4. Advantage #4: You get to learn "insider information" that can help you understand yourself and your clients and their situations better, thereby increasing the likelihood of successful intervention for them, as opposed to a hit-or-miss approach (This actually goes with number 2).

5. Advantage #5: As a qualified social worker you join the alliance of like-minded empowerers, justice seekers, and advocates on a global mission to better the world. How cool is that?!

What more convincing does one need?

More Convincing One Might Need

Not only are these advantages, but qualification in social work binds one to a code of ethics that guides practice, and this is to ensure that we don't damage the lives of others – or at least that we can do intelligent damage control.

This code, while embodying fundamental principles of how to treat others and how we should practice, represents unique characteristics not universally held by other professions, and qualification ensures that this standard of practice is upheld, but we'll talk more about that later.

A Walk in Their Shoes

Think about it. Would you want your child to be taught to play the piano by someone who may be nice, but who was unskilled in playing, teaching, or assessing?

Would you want your taxes done by someone who merely has a bank account, but no formal training in accounting – especially with all the changes in tax laws each year?

Would you trust your life – or at least several months of it – to a person who has a big heart, but who is not trained to handle all of the complexities that come with your teenage children, your aging parents, your stressful work environment, your mounting expenses and your challenges of self worth? Someone who may have a few good ideas, but whose ideas are subjective or disconnected from any tested solutions? Would you feel comfortable knowing that the person you choose to help you manage your affairs has not dealt with their own issues, which may be even more damning than your own? Would you care if that person acted completely independent of any standard of practice so that there was no way to hold that person accountable if, God forbid, they managed to screw up your case in some way?

Of course you wouldn't! So why would it be okay for you to "practice" on someone without being trained yourself? By the way, if you find you've answered yes to any of the above statements, you may want to consider therapy for yourself.

What Qualification is NOT

For a better understanding of this concept, let's look at what *doesn't* constitute as someone gaining competence in becoming a social worker.

You're not a social worker just because…

- You've watched every episode of Judging Amy and you know someone who has been abused.
- You've completed a 6 week certification course on Conflict Management in the Workplace.
- You've hosted a homeless family in your home for the holidays.
- You are part of the food basket give-away outreach program at your church.
- You made cupcakes for your child's class party.
- You've completed a few months of social work training.
- You visited a friend in the hospital after she delivered a baby.

- You've donated money to support Cartoon Art Museum or the most recent natural disaster
- You called the police because you heard your neighbors fighting.
- You collected old clothes from the 1980s and dropped them off at your local Salvation Army.
- You have a degree in psychology, psychotherapy, sociology, philosophy, spitballing, or anything other than social work.

Nope. None of the above applies.

From a qualification standpoint, none of these activities makes you a social worker.

~~~
*Smart Social Workers are qualified social workers.*
~~~

As a point of information here, I offer the social work certification requirements preamble from the Council on Social Work Education (USA) as to the standard for social work qualification and practice.

CSWE ACCREDITATION REQUIREMENTS

CSWE states: The purpose of the social work profession is to promote human and community well-being. Guided by a person and environment construct, a global perspective, respect for human diversity, and knowledge based on scientific inquiry, social work's purpose is actualized through its quest for social and economic justice, the prevention of conditions that limit human rights, the elimination of poverty, and the enhancement of the quality of life for all persons.[3]

---

[3] *CSWE, 2008 Educational Policy and Accreditation Standards*

CSWE accreditation standards require that the BSW curriculum prepare its graduates for generalist practice through mastery of a set of core competencies. These core competencies are measurable practice behaviors that are comprised of knowledge, values, and skills.

Social Work students delineate the educational goals and objectives of the Social Work Program through demonstration of specific competencies that serve to inform and aid evaluation of those students' preparation for generalist social work practice. These competencies serve as a link between what may be observed or demonstrated in student knowledge, value and skill performance, and the program's curriculum expectations. In a general way, these competencies and the practice standards operationalize the educational objectives for students, faculty, and administration and provide a common set of definitions to gauge performance and behavior.[4]

History, Anyone?

Social work has a diverse history around the world and is often linked with charity and volunteering, no doubt because the formalization of the field has its roots in the volunteer efforts of friendly visitors and charity organizations in New York.

Charity organizations were created to reorganize the public and private resources that had [multiplied] during the 1870s. Someone, though, had to perform the crucial tasks of investigation and treatment, and those "some ones" were the "friendly visitors", and what would be the social work profession was born.

The friendly visitors were women who were volunteers or missionaries and most from the upper class society. They strove to lessen the burden of the poor through direct service and prayer. The friendly visitors would first study and investigate relief applications, separate

---

[4] *For a complete list of the core competencies required by the CSWE for all social work graduates, visit http://resources.css.edu/swk/goals_objectives_competencies.pdf*

*the recipients into deserving or undeserving classes and then treat
them by making referrals and providing them with friendship.*[5]

Interesting....

Given the brief history above, let's consider some reasons why social work might still maintain its informal categoriza-
tion, shall we?

Friendly Visitors of the 1800's	Social Workers Today
Friendly visitors were friendly	Social workers are friendly
Friendly visitors were women	Most trained social workers today are women
Friendly visitors were volunteers	Social workers often volunteer

Notice a trend here? I do. And we haven't even mentioned that the salary for social workers has remained relatively
untouched since the 1890's. #kidding

Don't forget, we're still talking about Suzy.

So, what about Suzy?

So, what about Suzy? Is she a social worker or not?

I'm now going to make a statement that may seem to
contradict everything you just read, and it is this: Suzy is, in fact,
functioning as a social worker.

Confused? Don't be. It's really quite simple.

---

[5] *library.uncc.edu/files/4/sowk/word/History.doc*

Professional social work makes the argument that in order to use the title of Social Worker, one must be trained as a social worker. It's the same practice we use when we qualify doctors, lawyers, police officers and NASCAR drivers. If, somehow, Suzy is operating in a post with the duties of a social worker, though she was not trained as a social worker, she is, in fact, doing just that.

Consider this: can a nurse function as a doctor? Can a paralegal function as a lawyer? Can a police officer function as a detective? Can a NASCAR driver function as a taxi operator? In some instances, of course they can! Does the fact that they can function in another capacity automatically assign that title to them? No. No, it doesn't. It doesn't any more than having a sweet tooth makes you a lollypop, or a being called baby makes you a child. There's just more to it than that.

The fact of the matter is that social work is so much more than just doing good deeds or merely "helping" people. There's a scientific element to what we do – an empirically based standpoint from which we reference – and a legally binding standard to which we adhere. This is not fly-by-night nomenclature, or your grandma's home remedy.

Mind you, the nature of social work is such that the practitioner must use *self* as a tool for intervention. But even practice in the use of self must be molded and fashioned into a most effective device, and in order to maintain the integrity of the social work brand, must be done in a standardized way.

…wait a minute. What?

I said that the essence, the core, the basis of social work automatically requires that the social worker, in order to do his or her job, actually uses him or her *self* – just like a doctor would use a stethoscope or a runner would use his legs – a social worker's tool is their self. But, because there's a certain *way* that social workers use the self, social workers have to practice how to use the self to their best ability. And so, in order to maintain the standard, there has to be some agreed upon criteria.

Making sense?

The Final Word

Ok, one more time and for clarification:

1. The profession of social work operates from a specific framework and has a precise agenda.

2. In order to do this it uses a specialized set of skills, embraces an explicit knowledge base, and upholds certain values that set it apart from any other profession in the world.

3. The individual, then, that would practice as a social worker ought not only be aware of this blueprint, but must apply it in accordance with the objectives of the profession itself.

It's really a matter of standard.

Drum Roll, Please

And so, dear friends, the answer to the question that was asked is "**b**"; Suzy is *not* a social worker. It's only through enrollment in a program for social work education and completion of it – which includes some amount of practice under supervision from a more experienced professional – that gives you the internationally recognizable distinction of holding that title.

Does she perform tasks as a social worker?

Yes.

Does her experience in the field make her more apt to qualify as a social worker?

Most likely, yes.

Is she bound by the same set of standards as trained social workers?

Well, that one's tricky, because she cannot be held responsible for her practice in the way that a qualified social worker can, but because she occupies a post entitled "social worker", she should, at the very least, be aware of those standards and seek to follow them to the best of her ability.

Where Do I Sign Up?

And so concludes our lesson, dear one. If you are not yet a qualified, i.e. trained social worker, I do hope that you've been inspired to enroll in your nearest social work program today. And if you're already a social worker, I hope you've been affirmed in the legitimacy of your noble profession.

Every calling is great when greatly pursued. —Oliver Wendell Holmes, Jr.

Chapter 11

Ignore the Ethics

Live one day at a time emphasizing ethics rather than rules. – Wayne Dyer

Some Clarification

Remember in the last chapter when we made the point that it was important that anyone who wanted to use the term "social worker" needed to qualify themselves *as* one, and remember when we emphasized that the only way to qualify one's self was to receive a degree from a qualifying institution? And remember when we said that unless you do these things you cannot use the term "social worker" professionally?

Well, that's not entirely true.

Now, I'm not suggesting that I've lied to you – I just haven't given you the whole story.

You see, just as holding a gun doesn't make you a murderer, holding a degree doesn't make you a professional. There's just more to it than that. There's a standard of how we practice.

What is this standard, you ask? I'll tell you. But first, imagine being chauffeured by a person who was seeing-impaired, oblivious to his impairment, barreling down the side of a steep mountain road with no guard railing.

Scary thought, huh?

And yet, we might see trained social workers fly by the seat of their hot pants in nearly the same way – blindly leading their clients down paths of destruction because of their (the social workers') lack of application of appropriate attitudes and behavior; putting clients at risk of harm through unchecked actions and thoughts.

…and that, my friend, is why we have the Code of Ethics. It's a contract for the way social workers are expected to behave. Break the code, risk driving off the cliff of professional conduct.

That's the way it is.

True story

Now, I can't say that I see it often, but I know card carrying social workers who shame the profession with their lack of awareness and subsequent poor practice. I once knew a social worker who used to abuse her residential clients (emotionally and mentally). I met another who would misappropriate agency funds to pay her client's rent! Talk about good examples of bad practice! It's as if these trained "professionals" are singing from a totally different song sheet than the one assigned.

Mind you, I'm no social work saint by any stretch of the imagination, but while I can't say that I've deliberately gone against the code, let's just say that a blemish-free reputation on my part is questionable. It's been the code that has been my social work salvation and kept me on the straight and narrow.

Hallelujah for the code!

Enter the Code of Ethics stage right

If we were working with some sort of machinery or chemical formula it would be easy to develop, categorize and weigh every technical decision and/or action based on the underlying rules governing those things. But we're not dealing with those things – we're dealing with people and life. And the underlying rules we subscribe to are fairness, equality, and love – principals not always easy to categorize or weigh.

So, what's in a code?

A simple internet search will yield an extended version of most any social work Code of Ethics in existence, all very similar. It's this code that is used as the basis for monitoring practice.

...but don't take my word for it.

Around the World...

NASW (USA)
"The National Association of Social Workers Code of Ethics is intended to serve as a guide to the everyday professional conduct of social workers."

SASW (Singapore)
"The social work profession accepts the responsibility to contribute its knowledge and skills, to lend support to programmes of social welfare and endeavours to protect the community against unethical or incompetent practice in the social welfare field, which may be harmful to human welfare. The Singapore Association of Social Workers (SASW) subscribes to ...basic principles [of professional ethics] and requires its members to observe them."

BASW (British)
"The Association has a duty to ensure as far as possible that its members discharge their ethical obligations and are afforded the professional rights necessary for the safeguarding and promotion of the rights of people who use social work services."

JASW (Jamaica)

"As members of a profession whose authority comes as much a public mandate as it does from qualifications, skills and competence, social workers have an obligation to set out for themselves, those whom they serve, their organizations and the wider society, the values and principles which undergird the work that they do. In so doing they join the millions of other members around the world, who have similarly developed and are guided by codes of ethics or codes of conduct. These codes often serve as the basis for official policies and regulations governing the practice of professional social workers and members of the allied groups and disciplinary action can be initiated for breaches where these have been proven. The Code is binding on all members of [the] Jamaica Association of Social Workers, and the Association also hopes that its core principles and values will be extended to all social workers practicing in Jamaica and to their employers."

CASW (Canada)

"Ethical behaviour lies at the core of every profession. The Canadian Association of Social Workers (CASW) Code of Ethics sets forth values and principles to guide social workers' professional conduct. A code of ethics cannot guarantee ethical behaviour. Ethical behaviour comes from a social worker's individual commitment to engage in ethical practice. Both the spirit and the letter of this Code of Ethics will guide social workers as they act in good faith and with a genuine desire to make sound judgements."

My Take

I especially like the CASW'S acknowledgement that the code cannot guarantee ethical behavior, but that it comes from a social worker's individual commitment to engage in ethical practice.

"But Eva", you say to me, "what about the rules and regulations of my job? What if my boss mandates that I do something that goes against the code?"

Keep in mind that the code is there as a guide and supports broad principles of human rights, respect for self and others, and fair play. So if your boss goes against those things, you can either challenge his or her standard or find a job that doesn't compromise yours.

Ethics is nothing else than reverence for life. – Albert Schweitzer

Ode to the Code
By Eva Forde

A song for you, my faithful friend,

For your simple beauty to the end.

Dilemmas rise, but you stay strong;

The noblest outcome is your song.

And even those that think you trite,

Must look to you for wrong and right.

Your legacy of truth secure

Will ever guide my path, I'm sure.

I'm grateful for you keep me safe

In times when situations chafe.

Though sometimes you're misunderstood,

I rest and know your aim is good.

I love you, Code of Ethics!

The Code of Ethics

As I was saying before, social workers, having received certified academic training, are bound by a code of ethics whose general precepts are universal to social workers around the world. These principles guide the social workers' practice and, as they say, separate the men from the boys – or in this case the professional from the novice.

So, what's actually in a social work code of ethics? The International Federation of Social Workers (IFSW) and the International Association of Schools of Social Work (IASSW) – the two overarching bodies for social work practice and education internationally – have jointly agreed on general ethical principles that all social workers should follow. As a point of note, "some ethical challenges and problems facing social workers are specific to particular countries"[6] and so the following principles presented are general ones that, for the most part, appear in social work Codes of Ethics in some form or fashion across the globe. Hold on to your hats folks, 'cause it's a doozy.

Ethical Principles[7]

I. *Human Rights and Human Dignity*
Social work is based on respect for the inherent worth and dignity of all people, and the rights that follow from this. Social workers should uphold and defend each person's physical, psychological, emotional and spiritual integrity and well-being. This means:

 i. Respecting the right to self-determination – Social workers should respect and promote people's right to make their own choices and decisions, irrespective of

---

[6] http://ifsw.org/policies/statement-of-ethical-principles/

[7] The document "Ethics in Social Work, Statement of Principles" was approved at the General Meetings of the International Federation of Social Workers and the International Association of Schools of Social Work in Adelaide, Australia, October 2004.

their values and life choices, provided this does not threaten the rights and legitimate interests of others.

ii.   Promoting the right to participation – Social workers should promote the full involvement and participation of people using their services in ways that enable them to be empowered in all aspects of decisions and actions affecting their lives.

iii.   Treating each person as a whole – Social workers should be concerned with the whole person, within the family, community, societal and natural environments, and should seek to recognise all aspects of a person's life.

iv.   Identifying and developing strengths – Social workers should focus on the strengths of all individuals, groups and communities and thus promote their empowerment.

II.   Social Justice
Social workers have a responsibility to promote social justice, in relation to society generally, and in relation to the people with whom they work. This means:

i.   Challenging negative discrimination* – Social workers have a responsibility to challenge negative discrimination on the basis of characteristics such as ability, age, culture, gender or sex, marital status, socio-economic status, political opinions, skin colour, racial or other physical characteristics, sexual orientation, or spiritual beliefs.*In some countries the term "discrimination" would be used instead of "negative discrimination". The word negative is used here because in some countries the term "positive discrimination" is also used. Positive discrimination is also known as "affirmative action". Positive discrimination or affirmative action means positive steps taken to redress the effects of historical discrimination against the groups named in clause 4.2.1 above.

ii.   Recognising diversity – Social workers should recognise and respect the ethnic and cultural diversity of the societies in which they practise, taking account of individual, family, group and community differences.

iii. Distributing resources equitably – Social workers should ensure that resources at their disposal are distributed fairly, according to need.

iv. Challenging unjust policies and practices – Social workers have a duty to bring to the attention of their employers, policy makers, politicians and the general public situations where resources are inadequate or where distribution of resources, policies and practices are oppressive, unfair or harmful.

v. Working in solidarity – Social workers have an obligation to challenge social conditions that contribute to social exclusion, stigmatisation or subjugation, and to work towards an inclusive society.

III. Professional conduct

It is the responsibility of the national organisations in membership of IFSW and IASSW to develop and regularly update their own codes of ethics or ethical guidelines, to be consistent with the IFSW/ IASSW statement. It is also the responsibility of national organisations to inform social workers and schools of social work about these codes or guidelines. Social workers should act in accordance with the ethical code or guidelines current in their country. These will generally include more detailed guidance in ethical practice specific to the national context. The following general guidelines on professional conduct apply:

i. Social workers are expected to develop and maintain the required skills and competence to do their job.

ii. Social workers should not allow their skills to be used for inhumane purposes, such as torture or terrorism.

iii. Social workers should act with integrity. This includes not abusing the relationship of trust with the people using their services, recognising the boundaries between personal and professional life, and not abusing their position for personal benefit or gain.

iv. Social workers should act in relation to the people using their services with compassion, empathy and care.

v.　Social workers should not subordinate the needs or interests of people who use their services to their own needs or interests.

vi.　Social workers have a duty to take necessary steps to care for themselves professionally and personally in the workplace and in society, in order to ensure that they are able to provide appropriate services.

vii.　Social workers should maintain confidentiality regarding information about people who use their services. Exceptions to this may only be justified on the basis of a greater ethical requirement (such as the preservation of life).

viii.　Social workers need to acknowledge that they are accountable for their actions to the users of their services, the people they work with, their colleagues, their employers, the professional association and to the law, and that these accountabilities may conflict.

ix.　Social workers should be willing to collaborate with the schools of social work in order to support social work students to get practical training of good quality and up to date practical knowledge

x.　Social workers should foster and engage in ethical debate with their colleagues and employers and take responsibility for making ethically informed decisions.

xi.　Social workers should be prepared to state the reasons for their decisions based on ethical considerations, and be accountable for their choices and actions.

xii.　Social workers should work to create conditions in employing agencies and in their countries where the principles of this statement and those of their own national code (if applicable) are discussed, evaluated and upheld.

Not As Easy As It Looks

If you ever thought social work was for the faint of heart, think again. It's a consortium of technical and diverse, emotional and detached, and optimistic and pragmatic elements that, at any given time, are employed by fallible individuals with the sole interest of making life better for someone else. Admittedly, we don't always get it right, but you've got to admire our intent that always has the client's best interest in mind!

Just So We're Clear...

As you go through your social work journey, be sure to keep the following points in mind:

1. The COE is your friend. It's there to help you and protect you from "crazy" clients that would, otherwise, move in with you.

2. The COE is your clients' friend. It's there to help them and protect them from being taken advantage of by "crazy" practitioners that would, otherwise, take advantage of them.

3. The COE is not for decoration. It's meant to be used, applied, and lived.

Happy coding!

Ethics is knowing the difference between what you have a right to do and what is right to do. — Potter Stewart

Part 4: The Point

Chapter 12

Last But Not Least

Love is just a word until someone comes along and gives it meaning.
—Author unknown

Love sought is good, but given unsought is better.
—Twelfth night - Act 3, Scene 1

It Comes Down to This

Critical to our entire discussion and any true understanding of how to practice for ourselves or our clients is *love*.

(Crickets chirping against a silent background; baby screaming in discontent.)

A Hard Sell

I know. I know. It may sound corny and completely unoriginal. In fact, if you don't think it does, I'll go out on a limb and say that at face value it did to me until I got to looking seriously at this whole concept of love and started considering love as, not just an action or even an emotion, but as a force – as a powerful energy that could literally transform the world.

~ ~ ~

The Professional Social Worker knows that love is essential to the work that they do.

~ ~ ~

What's Love Got to Do with It?

I was first introduced to the concept of love as a force from *The Secret* (2006) that proposed the idea that everything in your life comes to you through a power called the Law of Attraction. As it turns out, the power is love.

Here me out.

Forget the categorizations, forget the philosophical postulations, and forget the pessimistic perspectives that might immediately come to your mind of what love is supposed to be. You know what pure love feels like. It doesn't need a justification or explanation or excuse – it just IS.

I Corinthians 13 from the NIV Bible says it this way:

[1]If I speak in the tongues of men or of angels, but do not have love, I am only a resounding gong or a clanging cymbal. [2]If I have the gift of prophecy and can fathom all mysteries and all knowledge, and if I have a faith that can move mountains, but do not have love, I am nothing. [3]If I give all I possess to the poor and give over my body to hardship that I may boast, but do not have love, I gain nothing.

[4]Love is patient, love is kind. It does not envy, it does not boast, it is not proud. [5]It does not dishonor others, it is not self-seeking, it is not easily angered, it keeps no record of wrongs. [6]Love does not delight in evil but rejoices with the truth. [7]It always protects, always trusts, always hopes, always perseveres.

[8] Love never fails. But where there are prophecies, they will cease; where there are tongues, they will be stilled; where there is knowledge, it will pass away. [9] For we know in part and we prophesy in part, [10] but when completeness comes, what is in part disappears. [11] When I was a child, I talked like a child, I thought like a child, I reasoned like a child. When I became a man, I put the ways of childhood behind me. [12] For now we see only a reflection as in a mirror; then we shall see face to face. Now I know in part; then I shall know fully, even as I am fully known.

[13] And now these three remain: faith, hope and love. But the greatest of these is love.

After reading this version I got inspired to write my own. Here it is:

If I get all these degrees, go to all these seminars and read all these books that supposedly make me more intelligent and marketable, speak at all these functions to people who sit very high up and are prestigious from all walks of life but don't have love, I'm just an empty barrel making lots of noise. In fact, I could even have the faith to accomplish great feats, but so what if I don't have love? What's the point? I can be as benevolent and generous on the outside as I want to. It looks good. It's what I'm supposed to do. After all, it's my profession. But if I don't love, I get nothing; it's worth nothing in the end.

Love is being patient - with me first. It's being kind to me first, then being kind to others is a natural outgrowth. Love allows me to release those things that keep me angry like envy and pride. It lets me breathe. When I truly feel love I am not rude — not to myself or others. When I recognize love I recognize that there is more than enough for everyone so I don't have to be greedy or get angry easily. In fact, love frees me to forgive and I don't have to be burdened with remembering all the wrong that was done to me. There is no record to keep! Love lets me seek truth and I love that! I praise that! I bless that! Love protects me. Love allows me to trust others and the power of itself. Love lets me believe the best about people and situations. Love preserves me and the good relationships that I have!

I can NEVER go wrong with love! Eventually predictions will stop. People will eventually die along with their talk and everything that they know. See, right now our knowing is limited. We don't see the whole picture. But when perfect love appears, everything else that's imperfect disappears. When I was a child I thought like a child and said childish things. But when I grew up I put simple thinking and reasoning behind me. I know we can't see and know everything now – it's like looking in a dirty glass. Eventually we will see everything clearly for ourselves. Now I only know part of the story, but I'm confident I'll understand everything completely, even as I am understood completely by God.

So we come back to these three: faith, hope, and love. But the greatest of these, the most awesome of these, the most powerful of these is love.

Feel free to pen your own.

Oh, What a Love!

I'm talking about a love like a parent has for their child, or a pet owner for their pet. It's the love an artist has for his craft or a player has for the game.

It's passion and compassion. It's energy. It's without pain, malice, jealousy, envy, or restrictions. Love, as they say, is a many-splendored thing.

The Science of Love

Still with me? Now watch this:

Researchers have scanned the brains of people in love and have made some shocking discoveries. As unromantic as it sounds, love is all science. Consider the following facts about love as reported by JohnTesh.com (yes, the entertainer).

Love is a Painkiller. A Stanford University study found that love reduces pain just as effectively as a powerful painkiller, like morphine. That's because when you're in love, your body is flooded with the feel-good chemical dopamine, which also reduces pain.

Falling in Love Creates the same High as Being on Cocaine. Researchers at Stony Brook University used scanners to measure the brains of people who had just fallen in love. The result? The areas of the brain associated with craving, addiction, and motivation lit up like crazy when they looked at a photo of their loved one, proving that we really are addicted to love.

Researchers also say motherly love makes your brain bigger. *Women were given brain scans before they became pregnant – and again after they gave birth. The result: The areas linked to motivation and behavior got bigger after they gave birth, and the mothers who gushed the most about their babies—like how beautiful and perfect they were—more likely to develop bigger midbrains than mothers who were less awestruck by their babies. So, falling in love doesn't just make you feel fantastic. It also acts as a painkiller, floods your body with feel-good chemicals, and boosts brain power. Three very good reasons to love more.*

Pretty interesting stuff, huh?

So now you may be asking the question, what does all of this have to do with social work? And I'm glad you asked, friend!

The Love Connection

When you love, you are, consequently, reducing pain—not only for yourself (if you happen to be in pain), but for your clients. This can produce a high that can really get under your skin and become addictive. Finally, you find your heart (brain) actually expands to encompass more people to love.

One is loved because one is loved. No reason is needed for loving. – Paulo Coelho

From a metaphysical perspective, love attracts love to itself and helps to heal the world of negative energy systems like anger, resentment, anxiety, and fear. That is to say, as you consciously choose the energy of love as your experience over negative energies, you actually bring more love into the world, and in the song lyrics of Burt Bacharach, "What the world needs now is love, sweet love."

Get this: in social work, love is not only the motivation that undergirds our practice, it is the intervention which directs us in all that we do as well as the goal we aspire to attain. It's the vehicle, the driver, and the destination. It's the runner, the race, and the finish line! It's the melody, the beat, and they rhythm! Feel free to use your own analogy here.

The Beatles may have said it best when they sang "Love is all you need." And if you intend to practice social work the way it's meant to be practiced, love *IS* all you need.

Stop the Presses!

Uh oh! Did that last statement offend your scholastic construct? I can hear the social work technocrats now shrieking in disbelief for my having "dumbed down" our noble profession. Not at all, my dears. In fact, far from it. If this sounds like an overly simplified strategy for intervention, please hear me out.

I'm not arguing at all that loving is always easy, or that it's simple, or that we don't also need ethical standards, a scientific knowledge base, or practice skills. What I am suggesting, however, is that every action we take is ultimately connected to the act of love at its core. Why else would we go through the trouble of scientizing the thing to begin with if we didn't believe that all people should be held in love?

When we talk about promoting social justice and equality, we're talking about love. When we talk about respecting the inherent dignity and worth of the person, we're talking about love. When we make it a point to honor human relationships, that desire is from a place of love. When we practice with integrity and make strides to remain competent, it's so that we can show love. In fact, our principle of providing service to humanity and our entire code of ethics can't be anything else but love. This, in fact, is our mandate.

> *This is my commandment, that you love one another as I have loved you.* — *John 15:12*

The Five Love Languages

Dr. Gary Chapman, author of *The 5 Love Languages*, proposes that there exist 5 categories in which we may express and experience love. These are through physical touch, words of affirmation, quality time, gifts, and acts of service. If we are not aware of how we understand love, or how another understands and experiences love, he argues, we might as well be speaking different languages, because the other person will not be able to relate to our version of love expressed.

How about it? Have you ever expressed your affection for someone that wasn't reciprocated in the way that you would? If so then you can understand how expressions of love can sometimes be misunderstood and discounted altogether, especially in cases where big egos and deaf ears get in the way.

Love in Action

For diagnostic reasons social work has needed to qualify how it demonstrates love through the professional and standardized cultivation of knowledge, values, and skills. But by now you may be getting a clearer picture of what it takes to practice genuinely including:

- ✓ *Loving yourself as a person of worth — an often missed and underestimated component*
- ✓ *Loving the process of bettering yourself*
- ✓ *Loving the inherent dignity and worth of each of your clients*
- ✓ *Loving the values that guide our practice*
- ✓ *Loving the pursuit of justice*

✓ *Loving the work to help improve people's lives*
✓ *Loving the lives you help transform and the futures you help to create*
✓ *Loving the idea of making the world a better place*

One of my former students put it best when she said, "Social work is love in action", and, indeed, it is.

What else would see social workers spending hours on the phone striving to obtain support for the single mother of four?

What else would have us spending hours researching, writing, and lobbying for policy changes for years on end?

What else would make us leave our comfort zones and remove a child from a home, lest it was the love of the rights of the child and the recognition that that right was being abused?

What else would have us continue to strive, day after day, when we know the salary for what we do can't begin to cover the much needed six week vacation to Cancun?

What else but love?

We cannot do great things on this Earth, only small things with great love. – Mother Teresa

To Be in Love

When you really look at it you can find evidence of this truth.

If you've ever been in love with a person or a thing, or have had a child that you love very much, you would have experienced the potent force that love has on your behavior, your outlook, and your motivations. You would have noticed that your love for this person or thing seemingly transformed your world; how you interacted with others; your energy levels; and your conversations. You especially would have been able to relate to the power of love if you've ever had your heart broken or your hopes dashed against the rocks of despair after losing something or someone you loved very deeply. It's almost as if the love that you had for that entity was life itself and now that that person or thing is gone you're not able to function in quite the same way you did before – at least for a period of time.

What We're Saying

So when I talk about love as a force – as a great power or energy or a spirit, if you will – I'm talking about love in its most potent form, which is really the only form there is.

It is your unlimited power to care and to love that can make the biggest difference in the quality of your life. – Anthony Robbins

Since I've bought into this idea, I've noticed subtle truths in songs and clichés from everyday life like:

~ *Love makes the world go round*
~ *Love conquers all*
~ *Better to have loved and lost than never to have loved at all*
~ *God is Love*

If love is such a powerful force, then it stands to reason that in order to do this work – working within systems, and with diverse people with challenges and challenging circumstances who don't always show respect, sometimes take advantage of you or the system, and are in constant need of support – then love must be a part of the skilled social worker's tools of engagement at, in fact, every level of intervention.

~ ~ ~

Smart social workers know that it's easier to love the work when you don't hate it.

~ ~ ~

Predictions

I'd wager that anyone who lives in fear, anger, jealousy, resentment, or hate is lacking in love, and that if they were able to open themselves up to love (which would require them becoming vulnerable on some level) and accept the love that is all around them in this moment, they would find that the fear, envy, jealousy, anger, and rage would melt away, and they would finally be able to enjoy life completely. In fact, I challenge you to consider your clients. I can almost guarantee you that most if not all of their problems can be traced back to a lack of love on some level.

Go ahead. Try it and let me know what you come up with.

~ ~ ~

Professional Social Workers know how to show love to their clients without losing their license in the process.

~ ~ ~

The Self of Love

If all of this love stuff sounds too difficult to pull off in your professional life, there may be a reason for that.

Professional social work uses words like "unconditional positive regard," "respect," "warmth," and "empathy" to discuss the concept of love, but it's all the same thing at the core, and it starts with loving yourself.

To love is to recognize yourself in another. – Eckhart Tolle

The concept here is to love one's self first and so much that loving others is a natural outgrowth of that experience.

If I love myself – if I love and respect my *self* – I will affirm that life force within my*self* that makes me the amazing, living, breathing, thinking, functioning human being that I am. I will value myself as a unique participant and contributor to this wonderful life, and in turn, acknowledge and respect the like role in my fellow human beings who may sometimes happen to be my clients.

Undoubtedly to some, the idea of giving so much love to self will seem very cold, hard and unmerciful. Still this matter may be seen in a different light, when we find that 'Looking out for number one' as directed by the Infinite, is really looking out for number two and is indeed the only way to permanently benefit number two. – W. Clement Stone

The Selfish Advantage

Let's take it even further. If I love myself, I will do those things that support my best interest. I will engage in activities that I love to do. I will eat foods that my body loves to consume. I will listen to music that I love, spend time with people that I love and who love me, and I will seek to create in ways that I love. In doing so, not only do I fill myself up with love, but the overflow of the love that I experience will naturally pour out to every area of my life, and this includes my clients and my work.

And how awesome is it to be able to motivate your clients—not from some theoretical text—but from your genuine understanding and loving of self? Pretty darn awesome, I'd say.

Years in the Making

In truth, the wealth of truth contained in this concept has taken me years to fundamentally embrace. But the more I study the subject of love, the more I am convinced of its unlimited power and unquestionable ability to transform any person or situation that may seem unconquerable.

Take a look at these scenarios and rate yourself on a scale of 1-10 to see if you are loving in relation to it or not. Remember, love is more than a feeling, it's also a force; but our feelings of love can help us gage the force at which love is operating in our lives.

Try the following on for size and rate yourself (10 being the highest) of how loving you are to yourself in any of the following scenarios:

Scenario	Score
If I've accomplished a major task	_____
When I've cooked a good meal	_____
When I've taken initiative on a project	_____
When I've overindulged	_____
If I've overspent	_____
If I've met an important deadline	_____
If I've broken a promise	_____
If I've disagreed with a coworker	_____
If I've had an argument with a loved one	_____
If I've watched several hours of T.V.	_____
When I'm late on an assignment	_____
If I've spent time with friends or family	_____
If I've overslept	_____
If I'm late for an appointment	_____

As a rule of thumb, if you score below 6 on any one of the above, you're probably spending valuable time beating up on yourself or engaged in some self-destructive or avoidant behavior when what you should be doing, in every instance, is forgiving yourself and committing to learn from your experience.

If you forgive every moment – allow it to be as it is – there will be no accumulation of resentment that needs to be forgiven later. – Eckhart Tolle

True forgiveness is a self-healing process which starts with you and gradually extends to everyone else. – Robert Holden

Don't Beat the Child

While going through my own process of self discovery, a very skilled friend of mine helped me to identify the childlike part of myself that was reacting negatively to a particular situation.

"What would you do for a little girl who is feeling the emotions that you are? Would you beat her," she asked me.

"No. I would show her love," was my reply.

"So why are you beating up on yourself now when it's your inner child that obviously needs love?"

Hmmmmm…. Good point.

For the Love of It

If you think about it, love is why we do anything we want to do. We buy stylish cars because we love the way they make us feel. We spend money we don't have because we love the results. In fact, love is even the reason why we DON'T do what we don't want to do! We neglect to exercise because we love to feel comfortable and avoid pain. We overeat because we love the way the food tastes, or if you're a contestant on The Biggest Looser, because you didn't get the attention from your mother that you needed as a child.

Whatever the reason, love—or the lack thereof—is paramount.

You will find as you look back upon your life that the moments when you have really lived are the moments when you have done things in the spirit of love. – Henry Drummond

And There It Is

I had an epiphany today. I spent the morning watching some life success videos and listening to Louise Hay. If you don't know who she is you can check her out and hear what she has to say about how to live an inspired, purposed life.

In her discourse on how to love one's self, she offered these thoughts that really hit home for me:

"I think it really starts with realizing that you don't love yourself — that most people don't. Most people feel they're not good enough, they haven't done it right, they won't do it right, they'll never be enough, and they're definitely not loveable. And when we come from that space, it's very hard to create things for ourselves that are really good."[8]

I would add that by contrast then, the reverse would be true; that when we come from a space of loving ourselves, accepting our goodness and recognizing our own capability, it becomes much easier to create very beautiful things for ourselves and for others that are truly magnificent.

The Final Word

Let us hear the conclusion of the matter. In Luke 6:31-34 from The Message translation of the Bible, Jesus puts the golden rule this way:

[31-34] "Here is a simple rule of thumb for behavior: Ask yourself what you want people to do for you; then grab the initiative and do it for them! If you only love the lovable, do you expect a pat on the back? Run-of-the-mill sinners do that. If you only help those who help you, do you expect a medal? Garden-variety sinners do that. If you only give for what you hope to get out of it, do you think that's charity? The stingiest of pawnbrokers does that."

…and that, my friend, is at the core of what professional social workers do—not some of the time, not when we meet clients we like – we do it all the time. We move in love. We speak in love. We act in love. We operate in love.

And that is *absolutely* how to practice social work.

---

[8] *You Can Heal Your Life, 2011*

I have found the paradox, that if you love until it hurts, there can be no more hurt, only more love. — Mother Teresa

About the Author

Eva Forde moved to Jamaica, West Indies from Brooklyn, New York in 2005 and subsequently became the head of the Social Work Programme at Northern Caribbean University – a position which she held until 2011. Prior to that, Eva received a bachelors degree in Social Work (BSW) from Oakwood College (now Oakwood University) in 1999, and a Masters of Science in Social Work (MSSW) from Columbia University. She has worked with the elderly, hospice, abused women and children, families in crisis, people living with HIV & AIDS, and survivors of torture. She also has a broad range of inter-agency experience in Jamaica and the United States.

Eva is currently the President of Jamaica Association of Social Workers (JASW), a senior facilitator with Pure Potential (*www.purepotential.yolasite.com*), and serves on the board of Human Rights and Democracy International (*http://www.hradi.org/home*). Eva is the founder and director of Positive Solutions International (PSI), a social interventions company that designs, implements, monitors and assesses social interventions currently in Jamaica.

Although her plate may seem to be full, Eva has expanded her methods of social intervention and has established herself as a performance coach for social workers, businesses and couples, helping people reach their goals and live life with authenticity and passion!

In addition to running PSI and being a coach, Eva is a dynamic public speaker and group trainer. A consummate student of personal wellness and development, she avidly presents on topics at the core of life success management such as Personal Mastery and Creating a Wealth Mentality. She is also available for motivating youth and adults in relationship and goal oriented issues. To contact Eva in the US call (917)579-7903. In Jamaica call (876)358-3994. Or email eva@evaforde.com.

Made in the USA
Lexington, KY
03 March 2015